# Enough

Enough

# Enough

MARIA MORALES

iUniverse

# ENOUGH

iUniverse books may be ordered through booksellers or by contacting:

iUniverse
1663 Liberty Drive
Bloomington, IN 47403
www.iuniverse.com
844-349-9409

Because of the dynamic nature of the Internet, any web addresses or links contained in this book may have changed since publication and may no longer be valid. The views expressed in this work are solely those of the author and do not necessarily reflect the views of the publisher, and the publisher hereby disclaims any responsibility for them.

Any people depicted in stock imagery provided by Getty Images are models, and such images are being used for illustrative purposes only.
Certain stock imagery © Getty Images.

ISBN: 978-1-6632-6892-1 (sc)
ISBN: 978-1-6632-6893-8 (e)

Library of Congress Control Number: 2024924489

Print information available on the last page.

iUniverse rev. date: 04/26/2025

# Introduction

I have known Mrs. Morales for a decade; we met here in California, though we're both from Mexico. I believe that everyone we meet has a role to play in our lives. Mrs. Morales is one such person. She has shown me that friendship and trust aren't just about blood relations or formal titles. She's a beacon of trustworthiness, honesty, and a supporter of education, always ready to assist without expecting anything in return—except, perhaps, for her students to learn, progress, and thrive despite life's challenges.

Initially, she was merely my children's tutor, but over time, our relationship evolved through warm conversations and her encouraging words, "Do you have time to read in English?" Now, as her student, I'm learning English, bolstered by her encouragement and academic guidance. Her life's journey, marked by both pain and tremendous joy, includes the triumph of becoming a teacher who writes not for accolades, but to impart wisdom and guidance through her words. To Mrs. Morales, I say:

"May books and writing continue to bring joy to your days."

My family and I are truly grateful to have met teacher and author Maria Morales.

Sincerely
Miriam Hernandez

# Prologue

Dear reader, I will share the story of my life, rich in details and information to aid your understanding. My family in Mexico lived in poverty; they aspired to provide me with the life they knew. My sisters were my pillars; through caring for and guiding them, I gained invaluable wisdom. Yearning for more, I made the decision to leave Mexico.

Enough is the name given to my book to bring light to such a dark secret that some women keep it hidden because it affects themselves and their loved ones. I am convinced that if a man ever raises his hand to harm a woman, it should be the first and last time. Remaining silent about such an incident is akin to a festering wound in the woman's heart. It is imperative that this secret is brought to light and made known. I kept quiet and hid the truth for twenty years.

Enough is the name of the book because women are human beings. Women should be recognized as victims when they are under a terrible situation like in a domestic violence situation. They seek to protect their spouses and their children, those beautiful beings born out of profound love. The law has what is known as a statute of limitations for reporting a crime.

Why should there be such a limitation for victims? When a crime results in death, no statute of limitations applies. A crime remains a crime. Indeed, I believe the same principle should apply in cases of domestic violence. I loved my husband; I didn't want to lose him! Ironically, he was the one who left me. He left me for a younger woman, twenty years younger than me.

I am not being swayed by emotions when I assert that the belittlement of women must end. The concept of family is beautiful, but sometimes, when a man abandons a woman, she becomes the family's leader. This is because the man has abandoned not just the woman, but also his children. We did not choose to be single mothers. I was committed to my marriage, but my husband did not honor our vows.

Whether single, divorced, or widowed mother, she is a mother striving to guide her family towards their goals, which are no different from those of a family with both parents. For mothers on their own, the challenges are significantly greater. Supporting women to become educated, professional, and devoted to their families is a vote for the family unit. To the parents, I say: allow a woman to marry whom she wants, when she wants. There is no need to conceal her completely; let her read, study, and if she doesn't wish to cook, she should not be compelled to.

Outdated laws must be reformed to ensure women receive full protection. This is not a plea for charity; it's a demand for justice. Women should have autonomy over their bodies and must be taken seriously during domestic disputes. These are not mere household arguments; they often involve an unarmed woman and a potentially armed man, creating a dangerous imbalance. Police intervention is crucial for protection. If women were assured of safety, similar to witness protection in criminal cases, they would be more likely to testify against their abusers, knowing they and their children are safeguarded from potential harm.

Therefore, it is imperative to amend the laws to provide women with equal protection, as they rightfully deserve to be shielded by the law. Historically, the correspondence between Abigail Adams and John Adams is significant. Abigail implored John to 'remember the ladies,' advocating not just for remembrance but for women's suffrage and political rights.

At that time, women lacked autonomy, legally bound to their husbands or fathers. This historical reminder prompts us to reflect: Have we progressed enough? In 2024, is there a need for transformative change? A change that fully acknowledges women as individuals with equal privileges to men, encompassing the right to marry, divorce, start a family, serve in the military, and make autonomous decisions.

I self-published five wonderful and terrific books filled with poems, short stories, and my memories. I've lived in two countries: one steeped in traditions with strict rules at home, the other offering the freedom to choose love or marriage. I chose love, having fallen deeply in it. At 25, I was no child; I was strong and brimming with life. Attending school in California bolstered my resolve to persevere. Though married, I yearned for more: a career and a family. I juggled a job, family care, and pursued teaching.

Despite domestic strife, insurmountable classes, and workplace challenges, I prevailed. I paused; my studies, awaiting a chance to resume. My husband's departure shattered another barrier; sending three children to college leaped another hurdle. With only two sons at home, ages 16 and 20, life seemed simpler. I handed my car to the younger and bid farewell to the elder.

Yes, this mother of two soldiered on. With no more barriers, the path lay open: work, school, and the pursuit were straightforward. The reward was within reach a diploma and a classroom of my own.

# My Memoir

I am composing my memoir as a retired teacher and author. I was born in Mexico and faced numerous challenges. I graduated from College of the Canyons in 2005, CSUB in 2009, and MSMC in 2012. I served as a substitute teacher for two school districts and tutored students in the afternoon from 4 to 8. In 2017, I began my journey as a Spanish teacher. The school extended my tenure into a second year, pleased with my performance.

Unfortunately, after 17 years of dedication to education, the Guidance High School shut down. The academic year of 2019 to 2020 marked my final year teaching. I retired in 2020 due to health concerns. Currently, I am penning my memoirs, following the self-publication of four books funded through my teaching career. This memoir, my fifth book, is intended to impart knowledge in my stead, as I will no longer be present in the classroom.

I've learned that the journey is better than the destination. My journey was so lengthy that I doubted my dream of becoming a teacher would ever come true. I never gave up and took one class at a time. For five years, I worked at several sewing factories in Mexico. I spent two years working in California onion fields, five years cleaning houses, four years as a nanny, and two years as a preschool teacher until finally, in 2009; I began working as a substitute teacher. My college classes inspired me to write poems and short stories in both English and Spanish.

I shared my writings with newspapers, and they were published. I shared them with my teachers, and they were well-received. Unknowingly, I spent my time immersed in reading and writing. My message to women is that education enables you to better support your families. Empowering women leads to the empowerment of all society members. Women are nurturers; they care for babies, neighbors, family members, and their nurturing extends beyond.

Love wasn't part of my aspirations; I was sexually abused at six, leaving me forever scarred. I harbored a fear of men. I never had the intention to marry, but I met a young man whom I believed was my prince; alas, he was not. After two decades of marriage, he departed for another woman. His loss! He left behind five wonderful children. They all attended College of the Canyons. Some of my children graduated and others did not, that is their journey, not mine.

**Wondering about my years working as a Substitute Teacher**

During interviews, the focus often lies on classroom experience. As a recent graduate, one may not have extensive experience, yet many teachers are hired right after completing their education. I've been told that my years as a substitute teacher count, but it's not quite the same. For seven years, I've longed for my own classroom, to know my students by name all year, meet their families, celebrate birthdays, and share in the joy of their progression from one grade to the next, witnessing the transition from elementary to junior high school.

I felt deprived of those beautiful moments, all in the name of experience. Talent often makes me ponder. Perhaps those administrators believed I lacked sufficient talent. But how does one measure talent? My five self-published books stand as evidence of my talent. One contains 100 poems, each a creation from my deep appreciation of the beautiful Spanish language. I have written over 300 short stories, some in English and others in Spanish. I rarely translate them; perhaps one or two, but my English books and Spanish books are entirely distinct entities.

Additionally, I've written and self-published three coloring books for children, inspired by my profound love for literature and young minds. Indeed, love, for I am their author. In 2011, a memorable encounter occurred as I walked alongside,

Dr. Paul A. Priesz, the principal of Valencia High School. Heading to the office to return a key after a day of substitute teaching, I mentioned to him that I had worked on that land 30 years prior.

He retorted that Valencia High wasn't built 30 years ago. In that moment, we were both correct. I hadn't clarified that my work was in the onion fields that once occupied the land where the school now stands. I transitioned from laboring in agricultural fields to pursuing a career in the field of education. Do you think working on the fields was a picnic? It was hard, so hard! History, dear readers, will eventually reveal the truth. Was Maria Morales overlooked due to a lack of opportunity, or was it something more?

I aspired to teach and feel deprived of my dream. I graduated at 56 in 2012. Was I too old to teach or too old to be hired?

My advice to college students is this: never surrender your dreams for anyone, and I mean no one. Your dream is your future, your life! My five beautiful books will teach. My short stories and poems will educate. I hold the title: Maria Morales, teacher and author, a title that lasts a lifetime, not just two years.

## Comparing Jenni Rivera' career with my own teaching career

While listening to the captivating music of Jenni Rivera, I found myself singing along to "Mariposa de Barrio." The title translates to "Butterfly from the Ghetto." In this song, whose lyrics she penned, Rivera shares her struggles to establish a singing career. As a woman striving to succeed in a male-dominated industry, she was not only beautiful and talented singer, but also a survivor of domestic violence.

Moved by her story, I composed a poem titled "Cantando con los Ángeles - Singing with Angels," reflecting on the hardships life dealt her, yet she was worthy of a path strewn with flowers. Her first husband was a bad man and he went to prison. My first husband was a bad man and he went to prison. She had five beautiful children. I have five beautiful children. Her family left Mexico. I left Mexico. We were two women living in California, each striving to conquer the world; one through teaching, the other through singing, yet both enduring silent struggles behind closed doors.

Tragically, Jenni Rivera, the renowned queen of Ranchero and Banda music, perished in a plane crash near Monterrey after a concert, en route back to Texas. A butterfly undergoes numerous transformations before it fulfills its destiny and flies away from the cocoon. Jenni and I are akin to butterflies; grounded, yet our gaze was ever fixed upon the stars, yearning for a better world for us and for our children.

Jenni Rivera aspired to fame and realized her dream. I never had the chance to meet her, but I did encounter her father, Pedro Rivera, at his event on Olvera Street in Los Angeles. I expressed to him my deep admiration for his renowned daughter; he responded with a warm hug and his gratitude. Jenni was blessed with a wonderful family who provided support throughout her career. Her entire family resided in Long Beach, California, her birthplace. As for me, I was born in Mexico, where my family still lives. Jenni Rivera beautiful songs will be always part of my daily life.

## Enough

The year was 1962. I was six year old, and didn't go to school. My two older brothers: Andres ten and Gil nine went to school. I stayed home helping my mother with my two younger sisters: Luisa was three and Susie was one. My house was an old wooden shack, consisting of a single large room. This room housed two beds: one for my parents and another for the children. Across from the beds stood a small table with four wooden chairs, a stove, and a wooden cabinet with a kitchen sink. There were no closets, additional doors, or a back patio.

The house was one of ten, forming a square with a central patio where the children played. At the end of each square was an outhouse; there were four in total, meaning some neighbors had to share the outhouse with one or two others. The side of the square served as the laundry area, with two large basins intended for washing clothes. Large wooden poles supported a hefty rope that could bear many loads of laundry. My mother spent long time washing our clothes, towels, the bed sheets and covers, and the dirty cloth diapers; the baby soiled every day.

The children frolicked in the central patio and ran around the sides of the square as they chased each other. They engaged in a game of hide and seek as well. During the search for hiding spots, one child discovered that the laundry area was an ideal place to conceal them. I stayed home, taking care of my younger siblings while my mother did the laundry, but as soon as my brothers returned from school, I went outside to play with them. In one of those times while I was playing with my brothers, one of my neighbors, invited me to his house.

He was going to give me some balloons so I could share them with my brothers. I knew him; he was the son of one of my mothers' friend. We played bingo so many times at his house. I went with him, and he gave me a balloon. We started chasing the balloon, around his house and he grabbed me with his hands and took me to his room. He raped me while covering my mouth with his hand. He told me to keep my mouth shout, and if I was a good girl, he will give me more balloons; I kept this secret from my family because I was afraid.

My father was working building a big steel factory that was going to house more than 2000 workers. The workers were supposed to work three shifts different times because the steel factory was going to be open 24/seven; meaning was to be open all the time. Big trucks with the material to be melt and then to be changed into big sheets of metal were going to be driving in and out of the factory all the time. My father was one of the lucky ones he went from building the factory for a year to be hired as a steel worker. The only requirement was to be able to read because, they must learn how to read the temperature of the giant calderas' or ovens were the steel was heated.

## My Parents didn't go to School

My father was born in 1926 and my mother in 1931. The Cristeros' war was ongoing when he was born, and his father had passed away before his birth. My research has uncovered details about the Cristeros' War (Spanish: La Guerra Cristera), a significant conflict in central and western Mexico from August 3, 1926, to June 21, 1929. It was triggered by the enactment of the Calles Law, which aimed to curtail the influence of the Catholic Church in Mexico. Notably, during the 1810 Mexican War of Independence, it was a priest who first rallied the populace to seek freedom from Spanish rule.

Mexican citizens cherished their Catholic faith and the Spanish language, yet they yearned for independence from Spain's control over their destiny. They aspired to establish a free nation. Today, Mexico remains predominantly Catholic, a testament to ancestors who instilled the belief in something greater than themselves: Jesus Christ. My family, despite their poverty, never abandoned their faith. I am profoundly grateful to uphold these magnificent principles, believing in something beyond myself and the world, in the Catholic faith.

Being the youngest of thirteen children, my father saw how my grandmother, widowed and with thirteen children to care for, managed as best she could. She delegated the responsibility of the ranch and animals to her older children while she remained at home with her daughters. She passed away in 1967 when my father was forty-one years old. I remember this because she prepared a delicious mole (traditional meal) for my First Holy Communion in 1965.

My holy communion in 1965 was a significant event for my family. My father was incredibly proud! His first daughter receiving Holy Communion was a blessing for us all! My godmother, who gifted me my lovely outfit, was our neighbor Maria. "Another Maria," you might say! Back then in Mexico, the name Maria was very common, often given to one of the girls in many families. Receiving this name felt like a blessing to me.

Let me share why my father didn't attend school. Besides being orphaned, he was impoverished. Owning a ranch that barely made money, the land and livestock only sufficed for their basic survival, not deeming education essential. However, at church, education was vital. The priest, facing the challenge of preparing children for their holy communion, found my father and some of his siblings illiterate. Undeterred, the priest resolved to teach them to read alongside their catechism lessons.

My father recounted this tale, mentioning the book used by the priest: El Silabario (Teaching reading through the use of a syllabus). My father's family was overjoyed after three months of learning to read and taking catechism lessons, culminating in their holy communion along with some neighbors. It's astonishing that in just three months, my father could read important documents, newspapers, and his beloved cowboy stories. I truly believe the priest performed a miracle, which is why my father was devout about attending church every Sunday and insisted we do our holy communion.

Despite the size of his family and the financial struggles, he ensured we went to school. My brother Andres did his best to help supporting my family financially after completing grammar school. He started working as a clerk in a small grocery store owned by my aunt Maria, my father's eldest sister. With no children of her own, she helped my father and, by extension, Andres.

He benefited from not having to deal with his younger siblings at home and enjoyed healthy meals cooked by my aunt Maria for him and her husband. She wasn't wealthy, but did her utmost to assist us. Every time she visited to drop off Andres, she gave my father some money. We looked forward to Andres' visits as he always brought the comic books my aunt purchased for him and the candy he managed to save from his share. My big brother was my hero!

My mother never learned to read because she opted not to go to school. Even though there was a school in the Rancheria where she resided, and her sisters went, she chose to stay at home with her mother. After finishing junior high school, I attempted to teach her to read, but she protested that she was too tired to learn anything and asked me to let her be so she could nap. It saddened me that she didn't want to learn to read, as reading was very important to me!

## Living in a Big House for the First Time

Andres and my brother Gil, they always share a twin bed. When Andres turned 18, we moved to a larger house with a living room, one bedroom, kitchen with a spacious pantry, a bathroom, and back and front porch. My father decided to convert the back porch into the kitchen, which then became my parents' bedroom. The pantry was repurposed as Andres's bedroom. The sole bedroom, originally designed with an en suite bathroom, was allocated to six girls.

Now the kitchen was going to be my parents' bedroom. The kitchen pantry was given to Andres to be used as his bedroom. The only bedroom that was originally designed as a bedroom with a bathroom inside was given to six girls! The girls were so happy, we never had a bathroom inside the house, and we got the bathroom! We were thrilled to have a bathroom inside for the first time. Although my mother and brother Andres were not pleased with the arrangements, they remained silent.

Ultimately, we were content to have a house without sharing walls with neighbors. My father enclosed the entire back porch with chicken wire and even purchased a door for it. Consequently, we no longer needed kitchen windows. Now, let me tell you about the doors in our house. We had a front door, a bathroom door, a door for the large pantry, a door for our parents' bedroom, and one for the back porch. You must remember the back door was my parents' bedroom door and the back yard door, was the new door my father purchased to keep the new kitchen enclosed.

However, there was no door for the girls' bedroom or for my parents' bedroom. In our unique family, the absence of doors was never an issue. We transitioned from a one-room dwelling for seven people to a spacious house, and no one complained about the lack of doors. The girls' ages were fourteen, eleven, nine, seven, five, and two, and we were all so slender that we appeared two years younger. My brother was 20; he deserved privacy and a new twin bed just for him.

The twin bed fit perfectly inside the pantry, but there was no room for anything else. He used the pantry shelves to put plastic bins on them. He used the plastic bins to put inside his clothes. He used one of the shelves as a table to put some of his things there. There was a little window at the top of the pantry, shielded by a wire screen but devoid of glass. My brother didn't complain; transitioning from sleeping in the kitchen to the pantry, he was quite content to finally have a door. Reflecting on the new kitchen, it was pleasant during spring and summer with its chicken wire enclosure, but winter brought some discomfort.

My father didn't consider it a hardship, as he grew up sleeping outdoors while tending to his lambs. We, city-raised, found it hard to connect with our parents' rural upbringing. Andres wasn't bothered by insects or dogs, unlike the girls who disliked both. The backyard boasted two fruit trees: a papaya and an avocado tree. We were fortunate that in our first year, the avocado tree was bountiful, providing us with avocados daily, akin to enjoying ice cream every day. Hunger was unknown in that big house!

The papaya tree, though small, only began bearing fruit in our final year there. Over six wonderful years, our already large family grew by two. My brother worked alongside my father at the steel factory. Occasionally, they would depart from our house together and stroll to the factory, a mere fifteen-minute walk from our spacious home. My brother, Gil moved to Michigan, USA, to live with uncle Perfecto. At fifteen, Gil left to work in my uncle's store, foregoing further education.

## Celebrating my Quinceañera

The year after moving to our new house was wonderful for me as I was about to celebrate my 15th birthday, a very traditional and festive occasion known as Quinceañera, kind of a sweet sixteen celebration. My father's co-workers signed up to participate as godparents, who are supposed to give the Quinceañera gifts symbolizing her coming of age. The gifts typically include a medal, earrings, a ring, a bracelet, a book and rosary, and a beautiful pillow for kneeling during the sacred mass.

In certain regions of Mexico, historically, women often married at fifteen. However, this was not the age I envisioned for marriage. My desire was to celebrate my Quinceañera with my family. At the time, I was in junior high with one more year to complete. My ambition was to attend high school and pursue a career in law. I extended an invitation to three classmates to be my 'dames quince,' yet only one agreed.

Similarly, I invited two neighbors; again, only one accepted. My father even asked a colleague if his daughter would participate, and fortunately, she agreed. Ultimately, I had three dames, no more. My mother said that my brother Andres could become my chamberlain, the young man designated to accompany me and dance the traditional waltz. Since I knew no suitable candidates from school, I accepted my mother's suggestion without objection.

## A Horrible Year 1972

The year 1972 could be considered one of the toughest for my family. I was sixteen years old, in my final year of junior high school, and looking forward to high school. Back then in Mexico, high schools were quite distant for students, often located in Monterrey, which sometimes meant taking one or two different city buses. My brother Gil was still in Michigan; he seldom wrote to us, and my mother would only call him once or twice a year. We didn't have a phone at home; we had to travel downtown to find a place where we could make a long-distance call.

After paying a small fee, we would ask the operator to connect us, and the person on the other end had to accept the charges. They always did, although occasionally my brother wasn't home. My mother frequently asked for money, unable to grasp why her son didn't send money every other month or so. I always accompanied her because she was illiterate. My brother Andres worked in the factory alongside my father. He never indulged in outings like dancing or dining; his routine was work and home, then work and home again.

He devoted his entire salary to assist my father and their large family. One February day, a car stopped in front of our house, and one of my father's coworkers approached our front door. Peering through the bedroom window, we saw the man. My mother answered the door and received news to rush to the hospital where my father had been taken from the factory. The man handed her a note with the details. When my mother was able to speak, she said we needed to go to the hospital.

Andres was at the factory working, so we left my thirteen-year-old sister Luisa in charge of my younger siblings. I instructed her to check the stove right away and to prepare a small meal for the children if we were not back soon. We returned at nine in the evening! At the hospital, my father explained what had occurred. He was on his way to a worksite when he experienced a severe pain in his back.

He collapsed, and his co-workers quickly came to his aid. He told them he simply couldn't stand up. An ambulance was called, and he was transported to the hospital. My mother couldn't stop crying! They performed X-rays, administered some pain relief, and informed us that we would need to wait at least two more hours for an update on his condition. After the doctors returned, they informed my father that he was cleared to go home.

They prescribed some pain medication and advised him to visit his primary care physician the following day for a back examination. Subsequently, we went outside to find transportation to go home with my father. Opting for a taxi allowed us to reach home more quickly and provided comfort for my dad, as his back was still aching. By the time we got home, it was already 9:00 PM. My sisters were crying while they hugged and kissed my father. My mother and I went to the kitchen to have a cup of milk, some cookies, and then we went to bed.

## Seeing the Primary Doctor

The next day, I arrived at the nearby clinic and waited two hours to secure an appointment for my father. When the secretary inquired about the illness, I mentioned his severe back pain. An hour later, my mother and father joined me at the clinic. They inquired about the waiting time to see the doctor, and I admitted that it was uncertain, possibly one to two hours. Although displeased, they took their seats in the waiting area. I stayed with them and while we were waiting, I was thinking about the first day that my mother told me to go to the clinic because one of my siblings was ill.

I was thirteen, just finishing grammar school and waiting for starting my classes at the nearby junior high school. Now, three years later, it was my father the one ill, my father the one needed to get well and return to work as soon as possible. Little I knew that it was going to need ten months for my father to be better and return to the factory. The doctor examined my father and his diagnostic was not very good. He told my father that he needed physical therapy.

The x-rays from the hospital showed something wrong in his backbone and the first step was stay at home take some medications and physical therapy. My mother could not scream to the doctor. She was going to scream at home. As soon as we arrived home, she began screaming at my father. He simply listened to her screams and told her that we needed to pray, trusting that God would continue to watch over us. They both started crying, and we, the children, joined in their tears.

Five years ago, my grandmother passed away, and two years later, my aunt Maria (my father's sister) also died. Aunt Maria was the one who supported Andres, and consequently, our family, since his earnings were for the family.

We children never discussed their illnesses; we were only told of their passing and we mourned their loss because we loved them dearly.

The entire family was frightened, and Andres was particularly terrified. At only twenty, the responsibility of caring for his family overwhelmed him. The next month, I had to attend a quinceañera for one of my friends; she was one of my 'dame's quince. She was also a classmate who introduced us to her sister, Nina, who assisted us with the waltz and the father-daughter dance.

Nina was incredibly patient and never sought any compensation. Andres told me that I must cancel the event, that they must know that our father was ill and I was needed at home to support my family. However, my father was not having an illness that could kill him. The possibility that he never could return to work was hanging over our heads. I complied with my brother's wishes, feeling that my own happiness was unjustified amidst the prevailing sadness.

## I couldn't go to high school

During his illness at home, he received half of his usual salary, which was insufficient for our large family of my mother and eight siblings. It felt as though my world was collapsing because he could no longer afford my books and school supplies. The application period for high school had begun, and my classmates had already signed up. I shared the sad news with them: with my father out of work, I couldn't afford to go to school. It was a terrible feeling, as if something precious was being ripped away from me.

Despite my own grief, I couldn't allow myself to cry or display my sadness; my father needed my support. A neighbor, whose daughter was sick, asked my mother if I could work for her. I spent two hours each day helping her sell food to factory workers during their lunch break, just across from her house. This job provided a welcome break from the turmoil and shouting at home. For six months, I worked with her, and she was kind, offering me a daily meal of rice, beans, and a choice between chicken or beef.

As soon as I arrived home, I handed the plate to my mother. She took it, and I didn't see it again until the next day when it was time to return it for lunch. I knew my mother would use the food to feed my father or Andres. That was fine by me; I didn't mind eating the same soup or potatoes she always prepared for us. Andres worked at the factory, while I stayed home, never feeling hungry. Serving food to the factory workers, I could smell the delicious meals, but I had no desire to eat them.

My thoughts were always with my younger sisters. I had to support my family; they needed to continue their education, have school supplies, and wear clean clothes every day. As I was learning to be a mother figure, my siblings were always my top priority. Every Friday, the lady I worked for would pay me 50 Mexican pesos, which I always handed over to my mother, never keeping even five pesos for myself.

At home, I had everything I needed: shelter, food, and family. The neighbor's daughters invited me to their church on Friday afternoons and Saturdays for a young girls' meeting, a sort of club that supported parish events. With my parents' blessing, I joined them. This gave me something to look forward to on weekends, in addition to attending church on Sundays.

Beneath my bed, I stored a plastic box filled with my old school books and the papers I received every weekend at church. We never had a Bible, but these papers discussed its teachings and included church songs. In a way, by repeatedly reading these papers during the time I wasn't attending school, I was educating myself on how to be a devout Catholic girl. My mother never removed my box, and my younger sisters learned to respect my belongings.

My father, once robust at 46, now walked with the frailty of age. A month into thrice-weekly physical therapy, we saw no improvement. Two months in, the routine persisted: I would arrive at the clinic to manage appointments, and then my parents would join to await the doctor's call. This was the state of medical services in Mexico fifty years ago, where workers and their families were insured by factory contributions to an entity known as: Seguro Social (Social Security).

Medical costs for doctors, therapists, and pharmacies were fully covered. Yet, beneath this seemingly perfect healthcare system lay a vast bureaucracy that burdened the very individuals it was meant to serve. Lengthy waits to see doctors and at pharmacies were commonplace. Urgent cases received prompt attention at hospitals, but otherwise, one could expect to wait hours for care.

Six months, after being taken from the factory to the hospital by ambulance, my father was diagnosed with a condition requiring a diskectomy, this is a major surgery. My father's symptoms included: Difficulty standing or walking due to nerve weakness. No improvement in symptoms after 6 to 12 weeks of conservative treatments like physical therapy or steroid injections. The intense pain used to spread to the buttocks, legs, arms, or chest.

The specialist advised that surgery was necessary to address his condition, with the risk of paralysis from the waist down, rendering him unable to return to work. My father, without consulting my mother, signed the consent forms for the surgery, which was scheduled one month later. Upon hearing the distressing news, my mother reacted with screams and tears. Throughout this challenging time, my father's faith, instilled in him by his mother, sustained our family.

Her teachings on prayer and unwavering faith never left him. The surgery was done and my father waited for three days at the hospital before going home. The doctor said that the surgery was an exit, and he was having a cast to protect his entire back. The rigid structure of the cast immobilizes and stabilizes the fixed disk and brings protection against dust and humidity. The family at home was so surprised when they saw our father coming home.

They were happy, but seeing him inside the big cast was overwhelming! My father needed three additional months after his surgery before he could return to work at the factory, bringing his total absence to 10 months. In 1973, at 17, I was at home feeling a big sadness without knowing how to help my family. One day while reading the newspaper, I found an add about a new school teaching sewing skills to young women.

I noted the address and, the following week, went to take the first class. Suddenly, I had the chance to attend a school that trained women to operate industrial sewing machines. They were massive and intimidating, but I was lucky to be learning a valuable skill. Upon completing the trade school, I began searching for jobs in sewing factories. There were so many sewing factories I Monterrey, some were very big and they paid better. Some were small and they couldn't afford good salaries for the workers. I quickly found employment at a small sewing factory, I wasn't 18 yet, but the factory didn't mind. They were in urgent need of factory workers.

# My Brother Gil Returned from Michigan

At 15, my brother Gil left home for Michigan. He came back in 1973, coinciding with the year our father returned to work. During his absence, he missed the challenges we faced at home while caring for our severely ill father for 10 months. I felt a bit upset with him but held back my words, as I was unaware of his living conditions in Michigan.

During the two years he lived with us, my brother was unemployed. He was ineligible to work at the factory because he was born in Texas, and only Mexican citizens could be employed there. My mother suggested to my father that they falsely register my brother as a Mexican citizen, concealing his American citizenship. However, my father refused to jeopardize his son's future by doing so. My brother accompanied me several times as I sought employment at Mexican factories.

Lacking a degree, I faced the prospect of factory work as my lifelong career, following in the footsteps of my father and my brother Andres. During the two years my brother lived with us, he would play football with the neighbors each afternoon. On one occasion, he failed to come home. My mother grew increasingly anxious, as he was never late for dinner. By ten o'clock, she was in tears, urging my father to contact the police. Where was her son?

The neighbors informed my father; they had played near the factory's perimeter, but had left without noticing my brother's absence. At nineteen, my brother appeared no older than fifteen; he was slender, clad in worn shorts and an old soccer jersey. My father approached the factory, informing the security guards, his son was missing. The guards reported that the police were called that afternoon after a teenager was spotted taking old wood from the factory's perimeter.

My father was incensed to learn it was his son. It was 11 at night when they had to head downtown to locate my brother. At the police station, they learned that my brother had been arrested for trespassing and possession of stolen goods. We all went to the station, and it was confirmed that he was there. Without the person in charge, my parents were powerless. They asked if they could provide dinner for my brother; the officers agreed, but only allowed my father to deliver it.

Outside the station, my father purchased tacos and a drink for my brother. Inside, he assured my brother that we understood the situation; he would return the next day. My brother explained that he had found the wood pieces on the ground and, thinking they were worthless, intended to give them to my father for repairing our front porch fence. He had not meant to steal, believing the wood to be discarded. Meanwhile, my mother wept inconsolably. She couldn't believe that her son was behind bars.

The American son was mistakenly arrested. The police were unable to assist my family due to it being Sunday, with no resolution possible until Monday. At the factory, my father was advised to seek help from the union syndicate first thing in the morning. The union planned to request the police drop the charges. An overzealous security guard had ordered my brother's arrest, unaware that he was related to two of the factory workers. Moreover, the charges were unfounded as the old wood scraps held no value to the large steel factory.

Following their advice, my father secured my brother, Gil's release from the police station on Monday morning, much to our family's relief, especially my mother's. My brother downplayed the incident, noting that the police had treated him well and that the other detainee didn't cause any trouble. After a two-year stay with us, he departed once more in 1975, this time to California, upon an invitation from our aunt Lena, my mother's sister. He never came back to live with us. His birthplace was Texas. While my parents had live there under, "The Bracero" program, my brother was born.

## We moved to our Own Home

In 1976, my father was one of twenty factory workers that won a house. This was kind of a lottery game without buying the lottery. There were 4000 factory workers. Already, more than 500 hundred had a house thanks to this lottery. Let me explain; every year since the factory was built, the owners gave the factory workers the gift of a house in December of each year. It was a gift, but the workers must make the monthly payments for ten years! The monthly payment was going to be deducted each week. I was five years old when my father was hired! Now he was getting a new house for us! We didn't have to move again!

My father never could buy a house from the bank. He didn't have any savings, bank account or someone to cosign for him. Winning one of the twenty houses was like winning the lottery! The name of the place was: Fraccionamiento Adolph Prieto. One of the owners of the factory was Adolph Prieto. The houses were not built yet. It was going to take three months to be built; the good news was that a grammar school was being built at the same time. My youngest sister was going to start first grade and my brother Jose was going to start fourth grade.

Our house was just one block from the new school! My younger siblings were very happy. My father was going to work walking. It was ten more minutes that before, but twenty five minutes didn't count, he used to walk in the old days two hours from the old shack to his job! Yes, two hours to go to work and two hours to return. When he had money, he took the city bus, but sometimes he didn't have the twenty five cents for the fare. He didn't mind: he walked.

My father was 50 and my mother 45 and they owned a house for the first time. The house had three bedrooms, living room and dining room together, kitchen and one bathroom. My brother Andres took one bedroom, the six girls took another bedroom and my parents took my younger siblings with them. For the first time each bedroom has a door, even the kitchen had a door. The front yard was small, but the back yard was big.

One of the sides of the house had a big space, and there was a build in sink with two spaces: one for wash and one for rinse. This was going to be the laundry area. I went to the furniture store with my father and bought a bunk bed. I was twenty and wanted my first new bed. I was going to sleep on the top and my two sisters took the bottom. An old full bed took part of the other half of the bedroom. All the bedrooms have closets and we start using them immediately.

The old kitchen table was moved to the girls' bedroom to be our desk. My brother was very generous buying a new stereo system inside a big furniture cabinet. We didn't care; we love to have vinyl records to listen to. The old TV was working, and my mom convinced my father to buy a new dining room and living room, nothing big, just six chairs for the dining room and a three pieces set for the living room. We used to watch TV sitting on the floor and my parents, using the old kitchen chairs. We felt rich!

The work schedule at the sewing factory ran from 8 AM to 6 PM, Monday through Friday. I had to leave home at ten minutes to seven and would return by seven each day. This routine continued for two years until I discovered a private Catholic night high school, Centro Cultural Lumen (Lumen Cultural Center), which was a blessing for me and exclusively for women. I went back to school! The tuition was 300 pesos a month, which I could afford, so I enrolled immediately. That evening, I shared the news with my parents, who remained silent.

Later, my mother confided in me that they needed the money to continue sending my siblings to school; two were in high school and two in junior high, all attending during the day. Despite this, I was determined to complete my high school education and experience that slice of heaven once more in my life. My brother Andres and I worked hard and contributed all our earnings to support our large family. A significant portion of the money earned by my father, Andres, and myself went towards my sisters' uniforms, books, and other school supplies.

## How the Adventure did Begin?

The adventure started when my brother Gil, who had departed Mexico in 1975, came back in 1978. After his return, I confided in him my plans to move to the United States. He offered support for any decision I made. My brother and my parents traveled to Guanajuato, Mexico, for two days. Unbeknownst to me, my brother was securing a legal visa for my father. My brother wanted that my father become a legal resident. When he left for California once more, he left me, his small blue suitcase, taking only the clothes on his back.

That year was eventful: my brother Andrés was getting married, I graduated from high school, and shortly after, I lost my job! I was given 10,000 pesos as a severance payment! In those days, I was making 800 pesos a week. The week was 40 hours of working time; I started working at 8 A M and finishing at 6 PM for five days a week. I started working at the sewing factory in 1974, when I was 18 years old. I dedicated four years of my life to that factory.

They fired three of the 40 workers. Their names were: Melisa, Luz, and Maria. I was one of them! For three months the three of us, worked on a plan to bring the union to the factory. We were supposed to meet at the union quarters every other day at 6:30 in the afternoon. When Melissa asked me to be part of the small group, I didn't hesitate because my own father was a union member. He had worked at Flat Steels factory, since I was six year old. My parents were so proud of me when I told them that I was one of the proud workers making petitions to the other workers to bring the union.

The benefits were awesome. They promised us the union was going to ask the owner of the factory for more benefits such as: better brakes, better sanitary conditions, lockers for our uniforms, and so on. Some workers feared termination, yet most signed the petition. Last year, we lost two friends. One worker, pregnant, repeatedly requested breaks from a supervisor. She spent six months of her pregnancy seated, sewing shirts continuously. Another worker, burdened by obesity and requiring assistance to stand, had her request for part-time standing work denied.

The union promised protection against dismissal to the three of us who initiated the petition. They deceived us! On the day the workers were informed that union negotiations were approved, we were summoned to the office. We received our checks after signing a waiver, relinquishing any further claims to benefits from the factory or the union. Exchanging glances, Melisa signed first, followed by Luz, and I was the last. A supervisor escorted us to our sewing stations, ensuring we took only our belongings, changed, and left our uniforms behind.

We were escorted to the exterior door to leave the factory. The other workers looked at us, but remained silent. I was the last one to leave. I had expected my two friends to wait for me, but no such luck—they had gone. Without phones, I didn't even know where they lived. I was stunned. It was 2:00 PM; I had my paycheck, but all I wanted was to go home and cry. I shared the unfortunate news with my parents. They suggested that perhaps Melisa and Luz had gone to the union headquarters. I doubted it; they usually waited for me, as they had done many times before in solidarity with our co-workers. The next day, after opening a bank account, I began my job search.

This time, I have the experience, but I'm unable to share it with anyone because the factory that let me go won't provide a positive reference. Fortunately, in Monterrey, there are hundreds of sewing factories. The downside is that without a phone, I must visit each facility in person to inquire about job openings. Luckily, some small factories are situated close to each other. On that day, I managed to visit three places, but the outcome was the same at each: no vacancies.

The next day, I resumed my job hunt on the streets. Venturing downtown, I stumbled upon a quaint café. There, I purchased a newspaper and scoured the job listings. I marked five potential jobs. After settling my coffee bill, I requested change to use a payphone. The barista, aware of my job search, offered their phone for one peso per call, with a three-call limit. I accepted and promptly began contacting factories.

Fortune smiled on me; a factory nearby was seeking someone skilled with industrial sewing machines. I assured them I'd arrive within the hour. Upon reaching the location, I discovered it was a women's swimsuit manufacturer. Undeterred, I expressed my willingness to learn and my quick adaptability. They did not seek references, though the pay was modest—just six hundred pesos weekly.

I started working at the factory the next day. The supervisor was very kind and explains the job to me. I need to make some small stitches to the top of the swimming suit. It was so easy, the fabric was so pretty and I didn't have anybody pushing me to make more and more of them. When I finished twenty of them, the supervisor took them and brought twenty more to be done. She didn't talk to me she just left the pieces and went to help somebody else's.

One day, as I was about to clean the machine before heading home, a young girl approached me. She said she was about to use the machine, so there was no need for me to clean it. I turned to her and asked, "How old are you?" She replied, "My name is Sara, I am fifteen years old, and my sister also works in the factory." She didn't look fifteen, she looked thirteen! She was so skinny!

Her sister approached me to confirm that indeed, Sara was her younger sibling. I bid them farewell as it was time for me to head home. The next day, back at work, my colleague shared with me, "I'm glad to see you, Maria. My sister Sara was fatally struck by a car yesterday while crossing the street and management is denying she worked here."

I embraced my colleague, expressing my deep condolences for the tragic accident. She implored me to reveal the truth, that I had encountered her sister the previous day and that she had taken over my duties as I departed. Overwhelmed with sadness, I assured her that I would do so. She lamented that her sister had been trying to catch the city bus when a drunk driver struck her and fled the scene.

It was a sorrowful day at the small factory; some workers wept during lunch, while others sat silently, their gazes lowered in fear of the supervisor. After lunch, my supervisor instructed me to visit the office. There, I was informed that my assistance was no longer required and received an envelope containing payment for the three days I had worked. The supervisor without telling me a word; escorted me to retrieve my purse.

In this factory, we didn't wear uniforms. As I departed, no one met my gaze; fear had gripped them all! I worked at this factory for only one month. I left the factory, but I didn't go home. I went to the nearest grocery store to buy the newspaper. Then, I went home, not to cry, but to open the newspaper and started searching for a job. It took four days, but I secured another job.

The factory was quite small, employing only ten workers. The supervisor was surprisingly young, possibly around twenty years old. The work was straightforward; we needed to sew t-shirts. My task was the final step: hemming each one. The shirts were small, likely for teenagers, and featured vivid colors. The supervisor would bring me ten at a time, and I'd wait five minutes before she returned with another ten. The weekly salary was 600 pesos.

My brother's Andres wedding was coming up and I must buy material for my sister's dresses. My sister Luisa already a skilled seamstress, thanks to the classes that she was taking downtown and that I paid for, was so eager to start sewing the dresses. She struggled for a year trying to find a job without any success; at seventeen, she had no experience and looked so young that I bet no one wanted to hire her, thinking she was only fifteen!

My mother insisted that I take her to the sewing factory with me, but I refused. My sister was a skilled secretary, and I believed she would eventually be offered a job in her field. Meanwhile, she was finishing her classes at her school for designing women's dresses. With seven of us, we couldn't afford to buy dresses often. My sister learned to design them; I would only need to purchase the materials.

A relative in California gave us a small sewing machine, which Luisa could use while waiting for her dream job as a secretary. My sister was a quick seamstress and the dresses for the wedding were ready on time! Luisa began working as a secretary at a public school a week before the wedding. We were all thrilled for her. At eighteen, she may not have had much experience, but attending the design academy and creating beautiful outfits for herself and our sisters gave her confidence and pride in her appearance.

Another positive development now that my brother Andres would no longer be contributing financially to the family, it was Luisa would step in to help. This was a huge relief for my father and me, as we were the main providers, and without Andres's support, we feared the others siblings might have to drop out of school. Living in Mexico always presented the same problem: the distress of knowing that our earnings were insufficient for my large family.

Three of us were employed, yet Andres alone earned as much as my sister Luisa and I combined. Our father was aging and could no longer endure 16-hour shifts at the factory. It was 1978, and having just completed high school, I faced the reality that college was not an option due to financial constraints, and the chances of finding a night school that would allow me to work full-time during the day were extremely slim.

At home, there were seven girls, and our eight-year-old brother, Jose. Susana, at seventeen, had one more year of high school ahead. Lisa, fifteen, was in her second year of high school. Marina, eleven, was concluding her sixth grade. Two others, Jose and Patricia, aged eight and six respectively, were in elementary school. Luisa and I, even though, they were not our children, felt a moral obligation to support them.

I also want to share about two remarkable composers and singers from Mexico: José María Napoleón and Juan Gabriel. Both rose from humble beginnings to become extraordinary talents in composing and performing their music. We, as Latinos, embrace these songs because they resonate with our souls and bring us tranquility. It's inspiring to know that there are individuals who have endured great suffering for love and from material things, yet have turned their pain into art.

Their songs, echoes the hardships many Latinos have faced. These are the songs I sang during my youth with my sisters. We never attended dances, but we did experience a concert. When the "Napoleón" concert was announced, I secured four tickets, and my sisters were ecstatic. Our mother wanted to join, but we feared she might spoil our enjoyment with her constant complaints. We opted for the most affordable tickets in the gallery. Although we traveled by bus, I could afford a taxi.

The concert lasted from 8 to 10 pm, and it was a magnificent evening for my sisters and me. We returned home by taxi as the buses were overcrowded. We got home at eleven o'clock. It was our first act of rebellion against our mother, but it was absolutely worth it. Every Sunday, we watched Juan Gabriel on the popular show "Siempre en Domingo." Napoleon is still alive, Juan Gabriel died in 2016. He was in Santa Monica, California; he came to give a concert to his fans. I never saw him in person, but I still have his albums and listen to them very often.

Andres had a grand and beautiful wedding! Luisa designed all of our dresses. We looked so stunning! The bride was too busy dancing all night to pay us any mind. My brother was so overjoyed that I couldn't bring myself to tell him we needed help overseeing the dinner. We were dressed elegantly, yet we found ourselves serving tables, clearing them, ensuring all the guests; were content. Throughout my life, we have had relatives visit us, including my cousin Hilda. She didn't attend my quinceañera, back in 1971, but we invited her to the wedding. She arrived on the wedding night to give my brother a gift and then left. I was told she was crying, but I never learned why.

The only family member from my mother's side who attended was my aunt Consuelo. The rest of the guests were neighbors, my father's and Andres's co-workers. On the bride's side, there were some neighbors, her parents, and one sister. The bride was only 18, not working or attending school. I knew that the wedding was very expensive. My aunt Consuelo gave my parents some money, and told my mother that if I wanted to go to Michigan, she was going to welcome me.

My brother Gil played an important role in our lives. He was the one that encouraged some members of our family to go to California with him. I was one of them! The following year; one of my mother's brothers Lalo was coming down to Monterrey in his way to Texas. My mother encouraged me to join his family. They were going back to Michigan, one of the lakes states, returning after a month vacation in Mexico.

Another of my mothers' brothers Perfecto was the owner of a store and a restaurant in the state of Michigan. One day, I visited the American embassy in Monterrey to start processing my passport. To my surprise, I received it the same day! My mother warned me to be prepared; she was uncertain whether Lalo would stay for a few hours or a few days. Suddenly, my uncle Lalo and his family arrived, and my mother informed me that he would be leaving, next day. I assured her that I was ready, and so was the suitcase given to me by my brother Gil.

I could only bring one book with me, leaving the rest behind was painful. I aspired to attend college, but I feared I wouldn't succeed. Without a job, attending classes was impossible. My working hours at the factory: from 8 to 6 left no space for classes. Consequently, I decided to accompany my uncle's family to Michigan. I departed from Monterrey, Nuevo Leon, Mexico in March 1979 and spent six months in Michigan.

## I Flew to California

Unfortunately, my uncle was unable to provide me with full-time employment. Subsequently, my aunt purchased a ticket for me to California. In September 1979, I joined my brother and my father in California, and the very next day, we headed to the onion fields. My brother introduced me to the boss as his sister in need of employment. The boss agreed and instructed him to start my training as I was the newest member of the field crew.

Working in the fields was a challenge for me, a city girl, not accustomed to the life of a peasant. I had never before witnessed people laboring on the ground. Some knelt, others stood, and only one person sat on a small stool. I chose to kneel, which brought me closer to the onions, allowing me to grasp a bunch, shake off the dirt, secure it with a rubber band from the ever-present bucket, and toss it back onto the soil. It may sound simple, but for me, it was a test of will – either I succeed at this or return to Mexico.

I looked around and noticed that there were more women working than men. In my group, there was my father, my brother, my uncle, and his two older daughters. The three of them were Mendoza; we three were Perez. The man in charge was named Don Lupe, and his subordinate was El Bronco. At times, it felt like I was in a movie—it was so surreal! There was a lot of shouting when they counted the boxes at day's end. El Bronco would walk along the rows of onions, announcing the number of boxes completed by each family.

The Mendoza, were one family; the Perez were another, and so on. Each box should contain 72 bunches of onions. As a child, in addition to reading, I enjoyed making lists of animals and categorizing them into domestic or wild species. These days, I worked bunching onions, which requires counting them. Each bunch should consist of six onions. We count the onions while picking and cleaning each bunch. After tossing the first bunch to the ground, I count the next as the second, the following as the third, and so on. Once I reach 18, I start counting again at one.

There was a small gap between every 18 bunches, so I knew that when it was my turn to place, bunches into the large wooden boxes, if I picked up four groups of bunches, I should have 72 bunches. Some people thought I was crazy. Why was I doing this? El Bronco would occasionally check my boxes to see if I had placed 72 bunches inside, and I was always spot on! No one followed my method! I didn't dare try to convince them, but they were so impressed that by the end of two months, I was managing to fill 30 boxes each day.

We were paid two dollars for each box. In the first week, I earned only $50.00, but two months later, I was making over $50.00 daily! However, not every day was prosperous. At times, we encountered bad luck; the section we were assigned to was unfavorable. The onions were either spaced too far apart or so large that we had to abandon the area. Then, we would be reassigned to a different location, like the one along the 126 freeway, known as the snake's land because of occasional snake sightings.

I had never encountered a snake, but one day, as I was harvesting onions, I sensed movement! I screamed and jumped up from the ground. My father and brother rushed over, both asking simultaneously, "What happened?" I explained that something had stirred among the onions. The other workers continued their tasks; to them, stopping meant lost time, and wasting time was not an option. El Bronco arrived and probed the area with a large pole.

He lifted a small creature from the earth and announced to everyone, "It's just a frog!" The frog was the creature that had frightened me. Laughter erupted around me, but it didn't bother me. I retreated to my brother's car and stayed there for some time. Despite my apprehensions, I had to work; my family in Mexico relied on my support. Three months into my job, my brother ceased working in the fields. It saddened me to see him go, but I was glad he found a better job. Born in Texas, it baffled me that he endured such dreadful conditions for five years. The fields had portable bathrooms, but no special facilities for women, some of whom worked through their pregnancies.

There was no facility to wash your hands or face, leaving you exposed to dirt all day. There wasn't even a designated eating area! Many workers resorted to using their cars as a place to rest during lunch. Like many, I brought my own food, including a 16-ounce water bottle and a ham sandwich, every day. Our work hours typically ran from seven in the morning to six in the evening. While we had time for lunch or breaks, some only took a 10-minute break in the morning and another at around one o'clock.

By 2:00 PM, we would see some men leaving the field to pick up their children and bring them back to work. It was only few of them, but it was disheartening to think of those innocent children coming to such a dreadful place. Back then, with children around and trucks arriving to collect the filled boxes, some women would start their drive home while the men remained until they had counted the boxes, after which they too could leave. I often wondered how long the Mendoza family had been in this line of work—ten years, or maybe more. I never dared to ask; I simply kept quiet and accompanied them home.

I needed to have a private conversation with my father and my brother. Why my father was here in California? My brother explained that my parents persuaded him to apply for a green card for my father. My brother wanted to please my father and honor him by providing him the way to become a legal resident. What my parents didn't know was that as a legal resident my father must live in America all the time. He couldn't live here! He must go back to Mexico.

He must take care of the house payments by going back to work at the factory. He must take care of my younger siblings. If my parents want to live in California, then how could we possibly bring all my siblings here? Our house in Mexico wasn't even paid off yet. My brother couldn't secure a place for the three of us, let alone for ten. Were my siblings expected to quit school and move to California?

That was out of the question! I couldn't allow my parents to make such a decision for them. Additionally, my cousin Margaret has been asking for her money back. Last year, my mother borrowed $300 from her to contribute to my brother's Andres' wedding. I couldn't comprehend how my mother planned to repay this debt without a job, and now I was living with the Mendoza family.

I suspected, they might think we intended to take their money! I assured my brother that I would repay Margaret as soon as I earned money working in the fields. I also asked my father to inform my mother that he would be there next week and to cease asking the Mendoza family for money. They've provided us with shelter and food for a few weeks, but they were not obligated to support us.

I didn't stay with the Mendoza family or my brother for very long; one month was sufficient for me to seek distance. While perusing the newspaper, I stumbled upon an ad for a room rental. After calling the provided number, the lady agreed to rent me the room on the spot. I paid fifty dollars weekly to reside in a lovely house belonging to a woman named Tilly. She was childless, and her husband, an older gentleman, spent most of his time fishing. She rented out a room because she felt lonely. I wasn't much company, as my time outside of work was spent studying.

There was a big urgency in me to learn the language quickly so I could leave the fields behind. I was enrolled in ESL classes alongside the two Mendoza cousins; I only exchanged essential words with them, such as "hi" and "bye." I had no intention of befriending them as my brother had. For some reason, I just couldn't relate to them! We had nothing in common; I had spent my entire life in Monterrey, while they had always lived in San Luis Potosi. I balanced school with work at a factory, whereas they had only completed elementary school and stayed at home.

They were fortunate that my uncle returned to San Luis and took the whole family to California. Since then, the two older girls have worked with their father in the fields, while the younger children attended school. Their family was as large as mine, with ten children and two parents. I already paid my cousin Margaret my mother's debt for last year and Margaret who was a secretary at a car wash was happy of getting her money back! She gave me a false smile while thanking me for paying the money. I hope this family never again lends any money to my mother.

My mother was used to ask my uncle Perfecto for money and never paid the money back. Therefore my uncle refused to give her more money. In school, I was placed in a third-level class due to my years of studying English at the high school level. I possess a large vocabulary but needed assistance with pronunciation to improve my reading in English. Six months after my arrival, I was already driving my own car. My brother, who was about to get married, had been driving his fiancée's car and sold his old car to me for $1000.

He also provided me with driving lessons, and we communicated in English rather than Spanish. The Mendoza family spoke Spanish at home, which hindered the parents and the two older daughters from learning English. I believed it was a mistake to live in California for over ten years without learning the language; it felt profoundly wrong. Once I began driving, I devoted much time to the Valencia library. Discovering this marvelous place was a true blessing! On days when the weather prevented work, I wouldn't go home.

With a change of clothes ready, I'd head to the library instead. I immersed myself in bilingual books to grasp the meanings of words translated for me. However, I wasn't just reading in Spanish; I was committing entire books to memory in English. I even found books accompanied by cassettes, which I could borrow for two weeks, then return and exchange for more. It was blissful— surrounded by books and cassettes, borrowing and returning, then borrowing again. To me, it was heaven.

# My Brother Getting Married

In 1980, I was delighted to learn that my brother was getting married, a fact that surprised me as I didn't even know he had a girlfriend. I was informed that a bridal shower was being hosted by my cousins the following week for the bride-to-be. At the shower, I met the young woman and greeted her with, "Congratulations, welcome to the Perez family," to which she responded with a bland smile and a simple "thank you." Her reaction left me puzzled; was she shy, modest, or perhaps she just didn't wish to converse with me? I knew no one at the party except for my nine cousins. I longed for the company of my books—they never fail to love me back.

Despite my reluctance to be among these people, I felt compelled to stay; I owed that much to my brother. I was chosen to accompany the bride, and in California, tradition dictates that a young gentleman must escort us. I was at a loss; I didn't know any suitable young men. My cousins, who seem to have a solution for everything, quickly offered their help. They knew a young man, who also happened to be our co-worker, and who would be more than happy to escort me. I felt uneasy! I had never dated back in Mexico, and now, due to my brother's wedding, I was expected to participate in a ceremony I had no interest in.

My cousins were shocked when I declined to be part of the ceremony. They couldn't grasp my predicament. "It's just a church ceremony," they insisted, trying to persuade me. They wanted to meet the following Saturday to look for dresses. I reluctantly agreed to join them. Upon arriving, I discovered several gentlemen were present, including my designated escort. He introduced himself as Jose. To my surprise, his name was José, and mine was Maria. Such an occurrence could only happen in California.

It seemed the young man was hungry because after visiting the dress shop, he invited me to dinner. Although he didn't have a vehicle, I had mine. We enjoyed dinner, and afterward, he suggested that since it was early for a Saturday night, we could watch a movie. He was very pleasant during dinner, displaying an impressive knowledge of Latino music and singing along to the tunes in my car.

I was elated; it was my first time going out with a man. At the movies, he kissed me, marking my first kiss. Unsure at first, I quickly found myself reciprocating as we kissed repeatedly. After the movie, we left in silence. I drove him home, and upon asking, he said he lived in Newhall, California, giving me the address. As we listened to the same melodies, he sang each one. It was unbelievable; he was just like me, knowing all the melodies by heart.

The following Monday, he surprised me with a visit while I was at work. He could only stay for a few minutes, but I was delighted to see him. However, I didn't see him for the next three days. On Friday, he came back and invited me out for Saturday. I accepted, planning to pick him up at his place at seven. After he left, my cousins just smiled at me, but I remained silent. On Saturday evening, I picked him up; we had dinner and went to a movie. He sang along to the melodies, just as happily as he had the previous Saturday.

When I inquired about his education, he mentioned he had finished high school two years prior and had no plans to continue. I was taken aback; perhaps working in the fields gave him a sense of job security. To me, this wasn't stability but a job fraught with challenges, particularly for women. I kept quiet, knowing some people prefer to remain oblivious to the truth. This time, he kissed me before going out the car. He invited me to come in; I went with him thinking that I was going to meet his family.

The house was dark, he opened the door, and we went inside. It was a small house. It had a living room, I could see the kitchen and the bedroom door was open. I was going to sit down, but he took my hand and guided me to the bedroom. It was his bedroom; he started kissing me and undressing me. I let him because I felt safe at his side. He put some music on while he left and went to his bathroom I stayed there waiting for him. He returned and joined me, hugging me and kissing me. It was lovely just as I read in my romantic novels.

He kissed me for few more minutes, holding me on his strong arms. He went inside me and I called his name over and over. It was a wonderful time for me. My first time! I felt so happy beyond any happiness experienced before. He finished and stayed by my side without talking. I wanted to hear his voice telling lovely words. He only asked me, "How are you feeling?" I answered him that I was OK. He said that this was not my first time. I told him that it was my first time. I never dated in Mexico because I was raped when I was six. He said that he was sorry about it, but it was hard to believe it.

The next morning, I saw him again. He approached me to inquire about the wedding, and I assured him that everything was set for the day. Our conversation lingered on music and dancing at the wedding, and I expressed my anticipation of dancing with him. He agreed, and then departed, not to be seen again until the wedding day. My parents attended, having been provided airplane tickets by my brother. My father shared how much my siblings missed me, yet he left out any plans of staying in California.

The wedding itself was pleasant; I shared two beautiful dances with Jose before he joined his friends for drinks. When another guest invited me to dance, I accepted, eager to enjoy the moment. My parents remained seated throughout, seemingly reluctant to engage with anyone. I understood their discomfort, knowing this wasn't Monterrey. Meanwhile, my brother was joyful, and the bride was preoccupied with preparations to depart the celebration. The wedding and dinner concluded in three hours, after which guests were welcome to stay, provided they covered their own drink expenses.

My parents returned to Mexico. My brother took a week off and visited Tijuana with his new wife for five days. I resumed work and never spoke to Jose again. Occasionally, I heard his melodious voice carrying a tune while he worked. One song spoke of kissing me and then forgetting me. I couldn't help but smile, knowing the song was meant for me. I wasn't going to cry; I had homework, projects to finish, finals to prepare for, and no time for tears. I persevered, working, attending my ESL classes, visiting the library, and sending money to my parents.

Occasionally, one of my sisters would write to express gratitude for the financial support and to let me know they were praying for my safe return. Aware that they were awaiting my return, I yearned to go back to that secure home, apply to college, and pursue a college degree alongside my sisters. At the end of 1980, I returned to Mexico for a two-week stay before heading back to California. I had wanted to stay in Mexico and return to school, but the money I had sent home while working in California was gone, and I had to go back.

My mother suggested I sell the car I bought from my brother. This time, I couldn't trust her. I knew that once the money was in hand, she would make plans for it. To her, our dreams of an education were mere fantasies. We were expected to marry and have a husband provide for us. Why didn't we share her faith? I couldn't bear to listen to her anymore; I grabbed my suitcase and left. Upon my return to California, I was determined to transform my life. I committed to working and saving money for my education.

A college degree was as vital to me as water is to the parched. Laboring in the fields or cleaning houses for subsistence did not deter me; my eyes were set on academia. Then, one evening after night school, a young and handsome man came up and said hello to my friend Lucy, who accompanied me. The man asked my friend out to the movies, but she declined, saying she was busy that weekend.

Surprisingly, I found myself saying, "I have no commitments this weekend." He smiled, and we exchanged phone numbers. It was the beginning of May 1981, just after the school year ended. Five months later, he became my husband. I was so enamored with him that I was content to live solely for him. My love for him was instantaneous. I had set aside my college aspirations, yet my life unfolded like a tale from 'Beauty and the Beast.' In it, I played Belle, striving to transform my husband.

He desired a wife who was both submissive and respectful. Despite my past mistake of having an affair with Jose, I was thankful that he accepted me as his wife. I vowed to manage all household duties, ensure clothes were clean, dinner was prepared, and contribute financially by working. However, attending school remained a necessity for me. After a year of marriage and twin children later, the monotony of domestic life weighed heavily on me, while he persisted in attending night school to improve his English. I discovered that he was involved with his teacher, which overwhelmed me.

He accused me of neglecting him due to my preoccupation with the twins, claiming he needed to dance and enjoy himself. His teacher, a delightful woman, was unconcerned about his marital status and sought only enjoyment. My husband insisted that as the head of the household, I should comprehend his stance. I confronted him with a choice between his teacher and his wife, reminding him that we were not in Mexico or Italy; this is America, and he needed to act sensibly.

I was contemplating divorce, shocked that the man I adored turned out to be a classic Don Juan, seeking fun while I cared for our twins at home. It seemed unreal. What was I to do? My family was in Mexico; my brother had his own family. He was fortunate to have a good wife who worked at a factory in Valencia, California, from 8 to 4, picked up their son from the sitter, then went home to cook dinner.

My brother was a devoted husband, returning home by six to dine with his family daily. Most of all my brother was a god citizen of this county, he never been arrested or committed a crime. I had longed for such a family life, but it appeared I had married the wrong man. The first time that I told my husband that I wanted to divorce him. He told me that he was going to kill me before he let me go. My life was a nightmare, but my beautiful children helped me bringing light into my darkness.

## Explaining Flat Steel Factory: Aceros Planos

I need to explain about Aceros Planos because the complete name of the factory was: Compañía Fundidora de Fierro y Acero división Aceros Planos- Iron and Steel Foundry Company: Steel division. Now, the workers just called the place "Aceros Planos", but indeed were two factories: Compañía Fundidora de Fierro y Acero- Iron and Steel Foundry Company was built first. In the year of 2016 both factories were shot down. More than 4000 workers sadly lost their jobs!

The declaration of bankruptcy by the owners left the iron and steel workers devastated. They had roles ranging from mechanics to supervisors; some were engineers, others were responsible for the cleaning and oversight of the factories, which were so expansive they required constant monitoring. I mentioned: Aceros Planos factory specifically because it was where my father and brother were employed — my father for 30 years and my brother for 16. The factory's immense structure was both vast and impressive, spanning an area of two miles by two miles.

My father was fortunate to be acknowledged for his 30 years of service at the factory, and he had finished paying off the house. He was set to receive his pension for life. In contrast, my brother was heartbroken because, after 16 years of work, he only received layoff benefits. He completed only grammar school and at 14, started working as a helper under the supervision of my aunt Maria, my father's sister, who passed away three years later. At 17, my brother didn't need references to begin working at the factory since my father vouched for him.

## 1986 was a Good Year in California

In 1986, I was living in California, married with three children. That year, one of my sisters called to inform me of the situation. She sought help because, without the financial support of my father and my married sister Luisa, the family couldn't afford the educational expenses for my younger siblings. One of my sisters was 23, the other 21. They also called my brother Gil for support. My brother Gil and I decided to support them, so they could come to California with a six months visitor visa.

They arrived to California and my brother was the one to take them to his home. He told them that they have to decide if they wanted to stay with him or with me. I was so happy to see my sisters; the last time was in 1981, when I left Mexico with a broken heart. Then I was lucky to find my prince and got married 10/16/1981. My sisters came to my home and they told me that the situation for them in Mexico was very bad. They wanted to work for six months and go back to Mexico.

One of my sisters has completed a year of college, and the other just finished high school and eager to attend college. I empathize with their struggles, as I faced a similar situation in 1979. They were not fond of staying at my home since it was situated in a rural area far from the city. I shared their sentiments about the location, but it was the only available place where we could afford a large house.

It boasted three bedrooms, a bathroom, a spacious living and dining room, and a large kitchen equipped with a washing machine and dryer next to the stove. A sizable refrigerator stood next to my kitchen sink, set against a backdrop of beautiful plastic counters. The expansive yard featured a lovely garden with a playground for my children, ample space in the backyard for my husband's trucks, and my car.

It was completely enclosed by a five-foot-tall plain metal fence with three openings: one for the house entrance, another for the garage, and a large gate for the trucks. Since they were not automatic, someone had to get out of the vehicle to open them. The rent was incredibly affordable at just 500 dollars a month, the same amount we were paying previously for a one-bedroom rental in Canyon Country.

My brother and his wife were married in 1980 and had already purchased their own home in Canyon Country. They managed to buy the house because my sister-in-law had savings, and also, her brother and his wife lived with them, paying rent. I was content living with just my husband and three children; I was pregnant with my fourth child and not employed at the time.

My two sisters stayed with my brother, and we began reaching out to our friends and those who employed my husband as their gardener. My sisters were fortunate because they both found employment within a week. They worked as nannies; one lived in with the family, and the other worked five days a week from seven in the morning to seven in the evening. It was my husband who secured a position for my older sister; he connected her with a family that had two children and working parents.

They resided in Newhall, California, a picturesque rural area with a spacious house and expansive tennis courts. The courts were large and well-maintained. My husband took care of the large garden surrounding the house and the upkeep of the tennis court. The family agreed to have my sister stay with them for six months. They also mentioned that they will be happy to take her to school in the evenings.

The father was a dentist who owned his own practice, and his wife worked as the office manager. They were both bilingual in English and Spanish and wanted their children to learn both languages. Every summer, they visited their respective parents, spending one month in Argentina with her family and another month in Spain with his. I admired the way they raised their bilingual children.

My sister, Marina, started working for a lovely family, caring for twin girls.

The mother was a lawyer, and the father, a school teacher. They resided in Canyon Country, close to my brother's home. He would drop her off at work and pick her up for school on Tuesdays and Thursdays. Both of my sisters, who were diligent students in Mexico, continued their serious studies in California.

They were eager to learn English to communicate with my family and their employers' families. Just two months after arriving, my sister Marina was already driving. My brother had given her lessons, and she picked it up quickly. Back in 1980, my brother taught me as well, and within a few months, I was driving his car. I didn't get the car for free; I bought it from him for $1,000.

My brother was generous with my sister, and through one of his employers, he helped her get a great deal on a car. With Marina driving, she could pick up Lisa, and they both went to school together. They were so content with their work and studies that they decided to extend their stay by six months. Their employers were delighted too, as my sisters were excellent nannies. Meanwhile, I was at home, caring for my four children, eagerly waiting the weekends when my sisters would go out.

They usually called me on Friday evenings to make plans for the following Saturday. They never stayed over because they wanted to go back to Canyon Country to attend church early on Sunday morning. I was pleased that they could go to church. With four children and a husband who always worked, even on Sundays, I spent my Sundays at home all day. I learned to sew little outfits for my two daughters and some nice outfits for my two sons, too!

Their ages were four (twins), two, and there was a baby. I was also busy cooking; they loved my chocolate cookies, muffins, and cheesecake. They adored my tamales too, but I told them tamales were only for Christmas. They were so young that they believed me! They enjoyed going to McDonald's in Canyon Country, and sometimes I invited my sisters to join us for lunch at McDonald's before we went for a walk around the beautiful Canyon Country' park.

The year went very fast and one of my sisters went back to Monterrey, Mexico. The other loved the family and going to school so much that decided to stay another year. I was happy that one of them stayed, I didn't have any more family members in California and having her here gave me great happiness. My children loved them because they played with them, chasing them around the park and read books to them.

While in California, my sisters chose not to date; they aspired to go back to Mexico and continue their education. Marina aimed to become a doctor, and Lisa aspired to teach. I envied them for their youth and freedom to shape their lives as they wished. Although married, I too missed schooling and had sacrificed my dream of becoming a teacher to be a housewife. I cherish my family, yet I felt profound loneliness. I was aware there was more to life than the ceaseless cycle of cleaning, cooking, and childcare.

With Marina gone, Lisa began to call me more often. Occasionally, when the children's under her care mother came home early from work, Lisa would seize the opportunity to escape to Valencia library. Then, she called me and invites me to have coffee at Barnes and Noble. I love the coffee there, but I never went back after I got married. I told my children to get ready, we were going to the library!

Lisa left the following year; she said that she couldn't wait any longer. She wanted to return to Mexico and attend college. She was 25 and for a Mexican woman this was like a warning; get your degree or get married. She didn't want to be married in California so far away from my other sisters and my parents. She left and I wished her the best. I saw myself in my younger sister. In a way she didn't want to be like me!

I was married with four children because my baby Kelly was only three months when Lisa left. For two years, I was very happy because my two sisters brought with them a piece of Mexico. Yes, a piece of a place that I missed so much, but I couldn't return because my children were American citizens and I learned to love this beautiful country like my own.

In the year 1986, my husband and I became legal residents of California, thanks to the Amnesty program. I am quoting from the internet, "The passing of the 1986 Immigration Reform and Control Act allowed for an update in the registry date. Registry in the United States is a stipulation within immigration law that allows undocumented immigrants to apply for permanent resident status if they entered the country before the established registry date and have remained in the country since, along with other specific requirements."

My son Henry was born in 1998. He was my last baby. Since 1986 I signed up my paperwork to have a tube ligation, an easy surgery for not having more children. When my daughter was born in 1986, she weighted 8 lbs and 8 ounces. A big baby for me such a petite woman! I lost too much blood and because of that my doctor couldn't do the surgery. He told me to return to Los Angeles, in three months and fill it up the new paperwork.

I didn't return and got pregnant again the following year. The nurse at Valencia clinic helped me with the new paperwork for a new petition for having my tubes tide. I didn't ask my husband! This was my decision. I love my children, but I was not going to be like my mother with ten children. When Henry was born, the doctor was able to operate me and at 32, I was told that everything was OK, I will never have children again!

When Henry was two months old, my sister Susana called me from Mexico. She expressed her desire to visit for six months, similar to what my other two sisters did in 1986. She mentioned she could only afford her flight to Tijuana and needed me to pick her up. I suggested she contact my brother Gil, as he was responsible for assisting our siblings. Susana relayed that my sisters had informed her about my sister-in-law's discontent at the end of their extended stay, and she preferred not to live with my brother, but with me instead.

This news took me by surprise, as I was unaware of these sentiments. I promised to discuss it with my husband, feeling elated at the prospect of seeing her again. Upon sharing the news with my husband, his immediate response was to inquire about her arrival date and to affirm that we would bring her to Val Verde. My sister, a recent medical graduate in Mexico, applied to a major hospital there. Although her application was accepted, she was informed that the waiting period could range from six months to a year.

With no funds for herself and our siblings, she urgently needed to earn money for our family. I promised to inquire about any available jobs in Val Verde. Despite only speaking Spanish and lacking a work permit, she was willing to work as a sitter or clean houses. Just like our father, she was ready to work hard; the necessity in Mexico was so pressing that she was prepared to do whatever it took. Just like that like a miracle my wonderful sister Susie was with me to help m with my five children.

We were going to baptized Henry and we were going to make tamales. I couldn't make tamales by myself. I was so happy that my sister was here to help me with such joyful event! The event was going to be delightful. My sister and I prepared many tamales; for our family and godparents family who also attended the ceremony. No one else came because my husband was not fond of parties. My children were thrilled when I invited the videographer from our church to record our dinner.

My husband had no objections, and the videographer joined us. At one point, he inquired about the attendees, and I explained it was just our two families dining together. After the meal, I encouraged my children to perform their school songs for the camera, preserving the memories. They put on an excellent performance, accustomed as they are to singing in front of an audience at school. I even coaxed my two-year-old, Kelly, to sing "Little Red Riding Hood" in Spanish for Aunt Susie. She did, earning a hearty round of applause.

In January, I registered for my inaugural class at College of the Canyons. My dear sister agreed to look after my five children. Every Monday for the next four months, I planned to drive to Valencia to attend my class. Although the class was only an hour long, I intended to spend an additional 20 minutes in the college library reading. My husband was supportive, and the children were happy because they adored Aunt Susie. Meanwhile, she secured a daytime job as a nanny for a family with twin boys.

The twins had roles in an English soap opera and worked in Burbank, California. Fortunately, my sister only had to care for one baby at a time while the other was on set filming. The family paid her a hundred dollars for the two days she spent with them on set. She was learning English at home, as my children spoke only English with her. She was fine with it, knowing that outside our home, everyone spoke English and she wanted to communicate effectively.

After six months, she got a call from Monterrey; the hospital was calling her back. She had found a job in Mexico and had to return immediately. My husband took her to the Los Angeles airport. I couldn't accompany her this time. On his return, my husband would work in San Fernando, so I stayed in Val Verde to watch her departure. My children cried, longing for her return. As a doctor, she was needed in Mexico.

My sister married at 35, having waited because she felt burdened, as if a chain were tied to her waist. She experienced the same profound moral pressure I did in Mexico, the stress of knowing our siblings might have to leave school without our support. She provided a sanctuary for Jose, our youngest brother, who never had to work in a factory. He completed high school and graduated from college at 23. Indeed, he was fortunate. He never worked at a factory and he never worked on the fields.

## Violence at Home

In May of 1989, we were talking about mundane things: the weather, his plants... Out of nowhere, he mentioned that a girl, fifteen years old, was crazy about him. I started crying immediately! He saw how upset I was, and he said that it was a joke! It wasn't his fault because; she was following him around while he was taking care of the garden. He was the gardener. I stand up and screamed: "I am leaving!" I started calling my children, we are leaving; I told them.

He hit my head with his own fist, and then, he went to the bedroom and returned with his rifle. I regretted with all my heart that I never called the police and reported him. I was afraid of him because, he told me that he was going to kill me, and kill our own children, too! He told me, the police opened a case against him. He could go to prison! I couldn't face my life without him. He told me that he was innocent. I believed him. I also told him to give the rifles to my father. He promised to do it because he said he would never hit me or threaten me again.

He had two rifles, which he used when he went hunting. We decided to leave California and moved to Mexico. I wanted to teach English and live closer to my family. I was so afraid that he could go to prison in California. I couldn't face a future without him. I have five beautiful children and wanted to keep the family together. I wanted to go to Mexico; I knew that my sisters could help me in this terrible hour of need. If he was arrested, I stayed in Mexico and my family was willing to help me with my children. I didn't want to be in Val Verde alone! I didn't want to be in California alone!

He agreed with me to go to Mexico and he promised me that he was going to give my father the rifles and that the he never could keep arms in the house again. The children were finishing school in one month. In that time, he could sell his garden service route, his trucks and tools. We were going to take two vehicles one car and one truck. He was going to drive the car with me and the children inside. His best friend, Pedro, was going to drive the truck with our belongings and the rifles!

## We are in Mexico

It took us two days to reach Monterrey, Mexico. My family was so happy to see us and meet, my children. My husband took his friend to the airport in Mexico and Pedro flew back to Los Angeles. Before he left, we gave the rifles to my father. I noticed some of my sisters were rare with me, but I thought that I was exaggerating. I wasn't wrong! I found out later on that they knew about my husband problems with the law and blame me to be involved with such a terrible man. We lived in Mexico for a month.

The children got sick, the business that my family promised to be very good: failed. We had lost 3000 dollars! This was because of a failed business with some of my relatives. Then, we got the called that our furniture was already in Laredo, Texas, and they needed to know the deliver place in Monterrey, Nuevo Leon. What a dilemma! We told them that we were going to be in Laredo, Texas the following day and get our furniture.

## We are in Texas

As soon as we crossed the border and the children saw the big McDonald's sign on the freeway, they started screaming: We are going to McDonald's! Yes, we took them to McDonald's and after that we went to a hotel. We slept, but we knew the nightmare was still going on! We rented a house in San Antonio Texas, and he started searching for a job. He went to the department of motor vehicles and registered our two vehicles as if we moved from California to Texas.

He found a job in construction and started working the following day. He worked only for two weeks because he was arrested in San Antonio, in September of1989 and I was left alone with five children. My mother and my sister Susana came to Texas to help me, but Susana had to go back to work and my mother stayed for a week. It was such a relief that Susie and my mother were with us.

Trinidad was in jail waiting to be taken back to California. My mother wanted to go back to Mexico even though I asked her to stay few more days. She didn't want to stay and I bought her a ticket. The children and I took her to the bus station. I gave her $100 as a thank you for helping me and told her not to lose it. The bus was going straight to Mexico and I wasn't afraid of my mother getting lost, she always could ask the driver to let her know when she arrived to Monterrey, Mexico. I have to stay in San Antonio, Texas; I have to take care of my children. Four of my children were attending school already.

I couldn't think of my life without them! My husband went back to California to answer the charges against him. Securing assistance for my return trip to California took three months, as I had to sell the truck and drive with five children. The family of my eldest child's friend planned to visit relatives in California over the winter break. I expressed my concerns about traveling alone to the child's mother and asked if my family could accompany them. They kindly agreed to help us and asked us to be prepared by December 21st.

## We Returned to California

We returned to California on December 23, 1989. We stayed at a hotel on Newhall Avenue as we didn't have a house. While reading the newspaper, I came across an article about Santa Claus giving away toys in Canyon Country, California. I called the sponsors to inquire if the program was still open since we had just moved to California a few hours earlier. They confirmed it was open and recorded my children's names and ages.

The next day, I called a taxi to take us to the event. Henry was almost two years old, and I didn't want to drive without a child seat for him. The driver took us to the event, and on the way, we began to chat. I mentioned that I was looking for a house to rent since I had just moved back to California. He said that his friend had called him the previous night seeking help with a house in Valencia. His friend had bought another house far away and couldn't manage the vacant property.

He had the keys and offered to show me the place on our way back from the event. I accepted, and he agreed to pick us up two hours later. The event made my children incredibly happy. They received breakfast, toys, enjoyed Christmas songs, and even took pictures with Santa! They were so delighted that they completely forgot we didn't have a home to return to. The driver took me back to Valencia to view the rental house. I agreed with the rental price, the deposit, and all the terms. I needed to move immediately.

The driver also mentioned that the owner had some furniture at another property on the same street that he was looking to part with. He led us to the house, opened the garage, and showed me the furniture that his friend was offering for free due to a need to sell the property quickly. He wasn't selling the furniture; he was giving it away! The furniture wasn't new, but it felt like a miracle to receive some pieces when we had none at all. They gave me the keys for the house and didn't charge me for the few days before the first in the name of Christmas.

The following day, I reached out to my brother-in-law who has been staying at the house we left in June. He informed me that our refrigerator was still in his garage and he could deliver it that afternoon. Additionally, he mentioned, "My brother has been detained at a Los Angeles prison awaiting his sentence." We decided to visit Los Angeles the next week to see my husband. I haven't seen him since September, when he was arrested in Texas.

In January of 1990, I visited the social services office seeking assistance. I explained that my husband was incarcerated, I was unemployed, and I had five children under seven to care for. They requested numerous documents: the children's birth certificates, my marriage certificate, car registration, driver's license, and house rental receipts, among others. I provided everything they asked for. I was eager to work, but with five children, my prospects seemed bleak.

Enrolling them in school was necessary. The school for three of them was just two blocks from our home. I needed to find a preschool for Kelly, while Henry had to wait another eighteen months to begin! Preschool lasted only three hours, and the other children's school day ended at 2:00 PM. Fortunately, I was able to enroll Kelly immediately, as her teacher was familiar with my family, having taught my twins in preschool back in Val Verde, California.

In February, my husband received a two-year prison sentence. He was credited for time served in Texas and was set to remain incarcerated until June 1992. The news brought me to tears. By June 1992, Henry would be three, Kelly five, Ritchie seven, and my twins nine. We visited him monthly, despite the distance. To protect them from bullying, I advised the children to say their father was in Mexico on business. The elementary-aged children agreed, while the younger ones were too small to grasp the stigma of a parent in prison.

However, after several visits, one twin revealed the truth to a classmate, and soon all their peers were aware. I reached out to the principal for support, emphasizing that my children should not bear their father's burdens. They deserved to be regular kids, to learn, play, and exercise at school. Thankfully, the school administration provided excellent support, ensuring my children were content and well-integrated, with a few close friends and abundant love among the siblings.

I cherish living in Valencia; in the afternoons, I would take the children to the public library, the next day to the park, and the day after to the pool. Everything was conveniently within walking distance! I managed to attend a night class at College of the Canyons; this was set to be my second class. My first class was back in 1989 when my sister Susana visited for six months. Having her was a blessing as I was overwhelmed with caring for my five young children. My neighbor in Valencia would babysit my children once a week and I returned the favor during her grocery runs.

But on the day of my final, she couldn't help. So, I brought my five children to College of the Canyons and headed to the tutorial center, where students usually get help with essays or math homework. Finding it empty, I sought an assistant and explained my predicament: I had to take my final next door, and my children needed someone to read to them while they waited. I assured her it would only take ten minutes. She kindly agreed, and after I swiftly completed my final, we celebrated with dinner at McDonald's.

# He Returned with Us

My husband returned to his family, he still told me that he was innocent. I never questioned him, I was afraid of him. We used to fight late at night because he wanted to sodomize me. I refused him, and run to hide in the bathroom, of course I was crying. He was upset telling me that I wasn't enough woman; for him. I needed to please him sexually; I refused to please him, but he was stronger than me and, he forced me. I never told anyone one more time, I was frozen with fear!

He started going to an evangelical church and that gave me some respite. He went in the evenings for group prayer and even to help his brothers in Christ to sweep the church for Sunday service. I refused to join his church, I was born Catholic and was not going to change to please him. I didn't believe that he changed; I knew that he was going to show the spots soon or later. My twins and my son did their holy communion in 1994. They were so happy all dressed up.

My husband took us to church, but he didn't come to Mass. We didn't celebrate at home. I bought a cake for the children, but we didn't invite anyone. He didn't want to be around people. My twins started going to Placerita Jr. High; for the first time, my children were separated into different schools. Three of them stayed at Meadows elementary, this school was just four blocks away from my home. I was able to find carpool in the morning for the twins. I was able to drop my three children at Meadows in the morning; I was cleaning houses in those days.

The lady across the street from Meadows school took care of Henry because his classes started until 11 in the morning. I pick up the twins after work and then pick up Henry while my other two children walked home. They didn't have to cross any streets. Living in Valencia was good because they built walkways to the school and to the children homes. Two years later the whole schedule needed to change. I was working as a teacher assistant at Newhall elementary. My schedule was from 9 to 12 every day. My twins were going to Valencia high school, my son to Placerita Jr. High, and my two younger children to Meadows elementary.

Once again, I was able to carpool my twins, then, took younger children to Meadows school, take my son to his school and then I went to work. Sometimes after work, I pick up my twelve year old from Palcerita and went home together. I was tired; I needed a brake before going at 3 to pick up the twins. In 1997, my husband was keen on purchasing a house in Canyon Country. We visited the property; it was an older home but boasted spacious front and back yards. It featured three bedrooms, two full bathrooms, a living room, dining room, and kitchen.

However, the house was quite distant from the children's schools. Our twins were fifteen, our son was thirteen, and the youngest were eleven and nine. My husband was undeterred. We were set to leave Valencia, as he had grown weary of the neighbors' constant complaints about his numerous vehicles and the frequent trips he made during the day, transporting plants to and fro. Neither the children nor I wanted to move. He didn't care.

## We Moved away from Valencia

We moved to Canyon Country on September of 1997. Managing the logistics for five children attending different schools has become a challenging ordeal. My son, the one attending Placerita Jr. High, was resistant to moving. Similarly, my children at Valencia High School were not keen on relocating. The younger ones, however, silently adapted to their new school in Canyon Country. The eldest, assigned to Placerita, planned to commute by city bus. My routine involved driving the twins to Valencia High School early in the morning, then heading back to Canyon Country to assist the younger ones.

Occasionally, on my return, I would spot my Placerita-bound child still waiting for the bus, prompting me to drive him myself. My husband was unable to assist with the morning chaos, as he left home daily by 6:30 AM and returned between eight and ten at night. I had a conversation with my son attending Placerita. I explained that he should wait for me until I finished dropping the twin so I could take him to his school. Occasionally, he would wait, but often he left early. His preference was to accompany me at noon. I was working two blocks away from Placerita. We did until the school raised concerns about his afternoon absences.

The next school year, I discussed with my husband the need for transportation for our three children attending Valencia High School. He suggested they take the city bus like everyone else. However, I reminded him of the red car; he had purchased the previous year with the intention of repairing it, but never found the time. I expressed my desire for one of the twins to use the car and insisted he contact his mechanic friend to fix it. Reluctantly, he agreed. Subsequently, one twin began driving, ferrying the siblings to school.

This arrangement greatly relieved me as I was working as a teaching assistant and attending evening classes – just one class per semester, but it was my passion to continue learning. Henry, my youngest, was having a hard time at school. He despised the new environment and couldn't seem to make any friends. His teacher referred to him as Enrique, which is the Spanish translation of Henry, and he detested it. He also avoided using the boys' bathroom, complaining that it was filthy. I often pick him up at lunchtime and took him to Denny's.

Those days hold cherished memories of sharing a pleasant lunch with my youngest son. There were no fights with his older siblings, no disputes between his father and me. After lunch, I would ask if he wanted to return to school, and he always said no. Unfortunately, he didn't improve from his chronic constipation issue. It was so severe that he once had to be hospitalized. I stayed with him that night, marking the first time any of my children needed to stay in a hospital. I was terrified. The next day, the doctors informed me that additional tests were necessary, including psychological and neurological evaluations at the children's hospital in Los Angeles.

I was hoping that my youngest son could get better, I took a month off from working that way I could monitor his health more closely. I took him to see some doctors in Valencia and eventually he gets better. He still was fighting at home when my teenagers stayed home not having school from high school. He wanted to be with them and bond with them, but the boys always told him that he was so spoiled to be with them! He immediately sought my assistance, and all I could offer was advice to ignore the boys, along with a promise to take him shopping the following day.

Keeping the boys away from Henry was a challenge, but it was my youngest daughter who began to bond with him. At the age of 12, she and 10-year-old Henry would spend afternoons in my bedroom, engaging in dress-up activities and experimenting with my old jewelry box and my small makeup collection. It was a relief that they were occupied while I prepared dinner. Meanwhile, my eldest daughter, at 16, was immersed in school and numerous extracurricular activities. As a straight-A student, I was immensely proud of her, and it didn't bother me that she stayed in Valencia with her best friend, Abby.

She was eager to celebrate her sweet sixteen, but I explained that her father was not fond of hosting celebrations at home. I mentioned that I would request Jason's mother to cater the party at the Valencia clubhouse. Since Johnny resided in Valencia, I was confident he would agree to rent the clubhouse using his mother's name. I intended to cover the costs for catering and the clubhouse cleaning deposit. The plan was for a simple gathering with six of her friends, without new outfits, elaborate celebrations, or party decorations.

Three of my children and seven guests were expected to attend. Jason's mother was responsible for catering the meal and acting as the chaperone. She would be the sole adult present at the small gathering. My husband had plans to visit Ventura that Saturday, and I assured him it would be fine, but insisted the teenagers stay because Jason was celebrating his birthday. This was a minor deception I employed to keep my husband from attending my daughter's birthday celebration.

It wasn't the first time I had to tell a white lie to support my teenagers. As a mother, I understood their desire to celebrate with friends, even though my husband still viewed them as innocent little kids. One of my twins was dating and I couldn't tell that to my husband. Telling him about this situation was going to create another big situation because he will want to meet the guy, and then ask him about his intentions. I didn't want any confrontations. I was so terrified of confrontations.

## He Went Back to Prison

June 17 was a bad day for us; my husband was arrested and was taken to Los Angeles detention center. I told my children that their father did something wrong and he had to answer for those charges. My high school children were having finals; they were crying it was so hard for them to understand this situation. They thought that after their father was release back in 1991, he couldn't go back to prison. They didn't know that their father was illegal!

I told them that they must go to school and do very well on their finals. They were going to finish high school and go to college. They left and I went inside to face my younger children. My youngest daughter was watching TV and Henry was still sleep. I was working in those days at a nearby preschool as preschool teacher in charge of 12 children three years old. Preschool teachers don't do a lot. They basically have to chase children all day long. For 8 in the morning to 5 in the afternoon. My feet hurt so much every day that I have to rest for 30 minutes before starting dinner.

We were able to hide the truth from Henry for three days. When he asked for his father we told him that he was taking care of a big job in Simi Valley. After coming from school every day, he looked at his father pickup trucks and started noticing something wrong. By the third day he faced me and asked me to tell him the truth where was his father? I had to tell him the truth, but I knew; he was going to be devastated. I told him that as soon we'll know something we were going to see him.

My husband was in prison for seven months, after that he was deported to Tijuana, Mexico. He was living with his mother in Tijuana, but he convinced me to give him the money to be able to rent a house. That way when I visited him with the children, we could have our own place. I agreed with him, and since March of 2000 he was able to move to a small house with kitchen and dining area together, living room, bath and two bedrooms. The house had a big patio where my husband could park his truck.

Sometimes, I was able to bring two children with me, but most of the time it was one of them. He was meant to be living in this house by himself, yet in June, I discovered he had been bringing a woman over to stay the night. I was devastated. It was hard to fathom that after making significant sacrifices to travel from Los Angeles to Tijuana, my husband was involved in an affair. He expressed his loneliness without me and the children, insisting that I should relocate them and myself to live here.

It was not unreasonable; I had no intention of moving my five Los Angeles-born children to Tijuana, nor was I prepared to leave my job as a preschool teacher to work there. He was utterly oblivious. I dreamed of raising my children in a happy family, but my husband, Trinidad, who had been in Tijuana, Mexico since February 2000, left me for a younger woman. He didn't just leave me; he abandoned our five children, who were nearing the ages of 12, 14, 16, and 18.

Henry, who was twelve, attended a nearby junior high school where he earned excellent grades. For a few months, he also went to a local Taekwondo Karate school, which he truly loved. Unfortunately, after my husband left us, I was unable to afford the monthly payments for Henry's martial arts classes. The instructor was fantastic with him, and although I sought financial assistance through the school's secretary, I was informed that no scholarships were available at that time. It was with deep regret that I had to inform Henry his classes were canceled.

I worked at a preschool near my home and told him that after coming from school and eating a snack, he could walk to my preschool and stay with me. He was thrilled with the idea, and I was delighted to see him arrive every day at 4 pm. The ten-minute walk was good exercise for him. My work hours were from 8 am to 5:00 pm with a 45-minute lunch break. Since it only took me 5 minutes to get home, I would go home to sleep for 25 minutes before hurrying back to work.

Twice a week after work, Henry and I would stop by Vons grocery store to pick up a chicken dinner, some fruit, and fresh bread from the bakery, which made for a lovely dinner for the kids. After asking them to save some chicken for me because I needed a nap, I went to bed. My feet were aching from walking all day! I wasn't eligible for government assistance since I had a job, a house, and some old vehicles.

I attempted to sell a few vehicles, but couldn't manage to sell the blue truck, the red car, or my minivan, which was fully paid off. Fortunately, the government provided medical assistance for my children, though not for me. Nearby, there was a place called Sam Dixon Health Center where I took my children when they were ill. When I fall ill, I was required to pay a nominal fee, but often, the kind secretaries waive it when they saw me searching for coins in my purse.

After my husband left, the business started to crumble. We owned the house, yet I was responsible for the mortgage payments. My husband wasn't only a gardener; he also did considerable construction work. A year after he left, I sold the gardening service route, his truck, and all the gardening equipment and supplies for $3,000. I used this money to pay the property taxes, vehicles insurance, and overdue mortgage payments.

Yes, I worked every day because we needed to cover our daily expenses, fuel the vehicles, and pay the monthly bills. My twins had part-time jobs at Magic Mountain and their wages were modest. I never could ask them for money! I still have Henry, Kelly, and Richie to support until they could attend college. My goal was to send all my children to college before pursuing my own education.

## My Twins went to College

My eldest daughter used to drive my son to school and work. They graduated from high school, and they were going to attend college. Their routine changed when she was accepted at Loyola Marymount University in Los Angeles, California. She was going to live on campus, and then returned on Fridays to work at Six Flags Magic Mountain in Valencia. Fortunately, I managed to provide her with a working car because the red car that she drove for two years was gone!

I purchased the car, last year as a replacement when my minivan started to fail. I explained to her that she would need to continue making payments on the car for one more year, but it was dependable enough for her. She took the car keys and departed. I remained, watching her until she vanished from sight. My firstborn, at eighteen, was now a woman in pursuit of her freedom and destiny. An exceptional student and worker, I had no doubt she would thrive in this male-dominated world.

At eighteen, I returned to school, graduating at twenty while toiling in a sewing factory from eight to six daily. But my daughter, an American citizen, had a different path. Despite having a father who lost his way, she had a remarkable mother who yearned to give her the opportunities, she never received. Upon entering my house, I found Henry and Kelly in tears while my eldest son was engrossed in video games. Ritchie was out back, working on his off-road racing motorcycle.

He often took it to the mountains in the blue truck to blow off steam. At 16, he was already a hefty 200 lbs, strong enough to manage his bike. After spending some time with Henry and my younger daughter, I retreated to my room to sleep, repeatedly questioning when this nightmare would end. The following week, my twin boy announced his plans to move in with his best friend. They were set to attend College of the Canyons and had secured an apartment in Canyon Country, a mere ten blocks from our home.

Shocked, I struggled to reconcile my love for him with his academic struggles. He was intelligent but too preoccupied with video games. Nonetheless, I embraced him, offering my best wishes. My son didn't have a car; he had a bicycle. However, his friend would drive him to COC. He intended to give me the house key, but I suggested he keep it so he could join us for meals and video games with Henry occasionally.

My younger daughter, resisted attending the designated school to begin her high school education, disliking the school, yet the school district wouldn't allow her to transfer. Richie, with only two years left to finish high school, contemplated dropping out to find a job and save for a car. I asked the school district for help and they gave me the phone number of a wonderful school: Opportunities for Learning. This school was designed to help teenagers with education issues such as dropping out of school.

I went to the school office and asked for help. The director of the school, Melody, was a wonderful educator. She listened to the big problems that my children were facing. She developed an educational plan for Richie. Fallowing this plan, he could graduate in one year instead of two years. She told him that with a high school diploma it was going easier to find a better job, and save for a car. My children grow up with transportation. My husband always provided vehicles for me and for them! Without their father with us, they were so angry with the world.

The plan given for Kelly was going to need four years. She had some bad grades and needed to improve them in order to get better. The school was just two blocks away from our place! They finally accepted the offer, and I was able to enroll them in their new school. This school was ideal because they didn't have to wear uniforms nor needed transportation.

Moreover, they didn't need to attend school every day! They only needed to meet with their school teacher two or three times a week. The teacher advised them one-on-one on the various options available to them. They took a packet home, completed it, and returned it to school. After returning the packet, they took a test to prove that they have acquired the necessary knowledge. The passing grade was seventy.

That year, I had lost my husband and my twins (went to college), and our family of seven had dwindled to four. In November, a co-worker inquired about my Thanksgiving plans. With the holiday approaching the next week, I mentioned we'd celebrate at home, though I hadn't planned anything specific—perhaps just some pizza or chicken for the kids. She had some knowledge about my family but didn't inquire further. The next week, to my surprise, a large vehicle pulled up in front of my house on the day before Thanksgiving.

Two burly men came to my door with four bags of groceries. As I opened the door, I was about to inform them they had the wrong address. However, they assured me the groceries were for the Morales family. They placed the bags inside by the door and fetched more. They returned with two containers, one filled with mashed potatoes and the other with barbecued meat. After leaving the food, they simply mentioned their church was distributing meals to families. I expressed my gratitude.

My children were thrilled to see the food already prepared for us. My twin son was unhappy; he argued that we shouldn't accept charity. I explained to him that it wasn't charity but a blessing from above, and I intended to accept it because I was weary of cleaning and cooking. I asked my younger children to clear the table in preparation for our meal. "But it's not Thanksgiving yet," they exclaimed! I replied, "Yes, but we have food for two days, so today is the first of our two days of Thanksgiving!"

Please don't mention December! I wish to forget those wonderful holidays that were once so dear to my family. I didn't prepare any meals, and the same was true for the New Year's celebrations. Without my husband, darkness enveloped me. I longed to vanish, to simply fade away, yet I had to endure, one day at a time. Once again, my children performed a miracle, bestowing upon me the strength to persevere. I realized how much I needed them, just as they needed me.

We were still a family of four; we had become the new Morales family. I attempted to sell the house for five months, and there were times we nearly succeeded, but unfortunately, the sale never concluded. My children and I spent weekends cleaning and packing. Unsure of where to move with my children, selling the house was crucial to afford a decent place. I started making phone calls to the few friends that still talk to us asking for their help.

I had to clear out numerous plants and items from my husband's collection in the garage. Eventually, I decided with my son that we should focus on discarding everything, as it was too difficult to sell items that were old or unwanted. We rented a storage unit for my son's motorcycle, our washer and dryer, and some smaller pieces of furniture. I managed to cover two months' rent and continued to hope for a miracle. However, the miracle did not occur. The house was lost to foreclosure, and we were given one month to vacate.

## Found a Friend

In February 2001, I lost the house that we had purchased three years earlier, filled with so much hope. Those weeks and months were dreadful. My friend Francesca, who had separated from her husband, had been residing in an apartment with her eight-year-old son Charlie for three months. Upon learning about my predicament, she offered me a place to live with her. For many years, my husband and hers had been close friends. Her husband was the one who drove one of my husband trucks to Tijuana.

My husband needed his truck to be able to have transportation in Tijuana and get a job because he could not return to California. After living with my friend for two months, she announced her decision to return to her husband, giving him another chance. She left and we continued to reside in the small apartment until the end of my friend Francesca's lease.

The apartment only had 2 bedrooms and two complete bathrooms, living and dining room together and a small kitchen. My two sons took the master bedroom and my daughter and I took the small bedroom. She was not happy at all! One day, I visited the apartment office and conversed with the manager. I explained that I was Francesca's friend and in need of a three-bedroom apartment for my two sons and daughter, who required their own space.

The manager provided me with a price list and mentioned that two units would become available the following month. Discussing this with my children, Ritchie, who was seventeen and employed full-time at a nearby lawn mower sales and repair shop, offered to contribute $200 to help. Kelly, fifteen, was working part-time, and Henry, thirteen, was a student at Arroyo Seco junior high school in Canyon Country. In January of 2002, we relocated to our new apartment.

The children were delighted with the place, but it was a struggle for me. I worked as a preschool teacher and assisted a mother with her young children two nights a week. She was kind, but I was exhausted after my day job. After three months, I informed her that I needed to be with my own children at home. She was sad to see me go but understood my decision. I was uncertain about what to do; the next month was November.

I confided in Ritchie that I planned to sell the blue truck. This truck held sentimental value for my children; my husband had purchased it in 1993, a year after his return from prison. It was the vehicle in which two of my children learned to drive. It had also been our transport for numerous visits to my husband in Tijuana in 2000. Selling it seemed like the only option. The sale would cover our expenses for November and December, as I was always short on funds. For January, I was hoping for a miracle.

In late December, we found ourselves working as helpers in the home of affluent individuals. As kitchen assistants, we washed dishes and pots following the guests' meals. My 17-year-old son Richie was tasked with serving drinks. I assured them he was 20, and they were fine with it, emphasizing that he wouldn't be drinking, just serving. They agreed to pay us 300 USD for three hours of work. I also brought my 14-year-old son Henry, not wanting him alone on New Year's Eve, January 1, 2003. While the wealthy celebrated at home with family and friends, we, the less fortunate, served them, also cleaning up afterwards.

That night, amidst their festivities, we received a call from my eldest son, who had enlisted in the American Army in 2001, wishing us a happy new year. We reciprocated joyfully, without mentioning our work. The earnings helped cover January's rent and keep our apartment. By February 2003, I enrolled in teaching classes, determined to become a 'real teacher,' as I told the counselor, not just a preschool teacher. True to my word, by 2005, I had graduated and was college-bound.

## Why I worked as a Live-in Nanny

To enroll in university-level courses, one must fulfill the necessary prerequisites. Completing these prerequisites at a community college can circumvent the higher fees of universities. Moreover, obtaining an associate degree may provide better job opportunities while working towards a bachelor's degree. However, I couldn't follow this route because I needed to help Henry. At sixteen, he was preparing to attend classes at College of the Canyons. He was also going to work at Target in Valencia, California. He required transportation to attend school and going to work.

I was so proud of my son! Working as a live-in nanny, I was able to provide transportation for my son. While working as a nanny, I was able to attend my online classes, complete homework, conduct research for projects, communicate with classmates, and receive support for my math courses. The five- year child I cared for was in a kindergarten class at Castaic elementary in Castaic, California. The school was a block away from their house. I was hired as a nanny, but I was not going to clean, cook, or do laundry.

My certificate from College of the Canyons in Valencia impressed the family so much that they hired immediately. They told me that I needed to help him with homework, be ready to go to school and pick him up if he wanted to go home, and so on. They also told me that later on, he was going to do activities in the afternoon. I agreed with everything, but insisted in taking him to the park after homework.

Twice a week, in the afternoon, I took the city bus to cook for my children at home. At 10:00 PM, I would ask Henry to drive me back to work. Henry, tired would disagree. When I suggested going back using my car, he promptly offered to take me. I was responsible of the car payments, our insurance and give him gas money. Additionally, I covered the rent, groceries, laundry every Saturday, and the apartment bills.

At the time, Henry was 16 and Ritchie was 20. Kelly had left as soon as she turned eighteen. Both of my sons worked and attended College of the Canyons in Valencia. Ritchie contribute $200 a month to our expenses. They shared the master bedroom while I had a small bedroom with an en suite bathroom. All three of us were working, studding, and striving to become professionals. While they attended College of the Canyons, I pursed my studies at California State University, Bakersfield.

Some classes were on site, whole others were online classes. The professors from California State University, Bakersfield travel from Bakersfield to Valencia because the university shared campus at College of the Canyons. Henry was able to help me technology and computers guidance because he was having classes on those subjects. Years later, I helped him with his science class because I took the class first.

Richie was able to help both of us with my car because he was a good mechanic. While growing up Ritchie was always helping his father, repairing our own cars and trucks, therefore he learned good mechanic skills. Sometimes we saw each other once or twice a week, our schedules were so different, but we manage, to call each other almost every day! We never talked about their father, the pain never went away!

Henry started taking classes at California State Channel Islands University. He was also working in Valencia the weekends. Ritchie left me because he moved in with his beautiful girlfriend, Michelle. He used to come twice a week to Valencia to attend College of the Canyons. His girlfriend was also taking classes and working as a secretary in Los Angeles.

The Morales family wishes to pay tribute to College of the Canyons, Valencia, and the beautiful state of California. Records at College of the Canyons show that my five children and I attended classes at this community college. I was the only one to graduate with an Associate of Arts from there. Henry transferred to California State Channel Islands University. Kelly moved to Simi Valley Community College and earned her degree there.

My daughter, Rose, took summer courses while she was a student at Loyola Marymount University and graduated in 2004. My dear son, Trinidad Morales Jr., completed some courses, but in September 2001, a week before 9/11, he enlisted in the Armed Forces. My children hold Valencia and California dear to their hearts. They are my pride and joy. I regret the times I left them on their own because I was so passionate about books and education.

## Working as a substitute teacher and taking classes at Mount Saint Mary's University

I graduated from California State University, Bakersfield in 2009 and I started working as a substitute teacher for Hart school district and Palmdale school district in the same year. In June of the same year, I began my classes at Mount Saint Mary's University, a predominantly women's Catholic college. I was comfortable with my decision as the classes were online, scheduled for two nights a week and some weekends.

In 2010, I was completing my first year of graduate school, aiming to become a Spanish language teacher. I embarked on this journey with two classmates who shared my eagerness to teach. We undertook numerous projects to demonstrate our capability to instruct students in a foreign language. All three of us were native Spanish speakers: Emma from Cuba, Carlos from Puerto Rico, and I was from Mexico. Our teachers affectionately dubbed us 'the United Nations' students' as we aspired to impart the language, culture, and ancient traditions of our forebears.

Carlos, the youngest among us at twenty-five, worked as a teacher's assistant during the day. Emma, at forty, had spent two decades as a secretary, and I, at fifty-two, served as a substitute teacher. Despite our full-time jobs, we attended classes three evenings a week, driven by our dreams. The program's academic standards were rigorous, requiring a minimum 3.0 GPA to remain enrolled—a prospect that daunted me, given my undergraduate record.

However, I heeded the sage advice of a high school teacher: "Maria, ensure your teachers know you, participate actively in class, and seek help when needed." This counsel proved invaluable when I encountered a significant challenge in one of my courses. The course was linguistics, and I needed to complete a project and present it to the class. However, due to personal difficulties at home, including a divorce and relocating to a new city, I couldn't finish the project.

I explained to my linguistics professor that I had sufficient information for the presentation but not for the report submission. She asked, "Maria, would two months be enough to complete your project?" and assigned me an incomplete grade, which didn't impact my GPA, allowing me to finish my first year. Shortly before the school year ended, I learned that Emma had failed the linguistics class and wouldn't be returning the next year. When I inquired about her plans, she replied, "Sometimes it's better to stop dreaming; I'm going home."

Carlos passed his courses but decided to switch his major to Special Education instead of Spanish, inspired by his desire to assist his brother with special needs and other similar students. My first year ended on a somber note as a prospective Spanish teacher; I was the only one from my group returning to the teaching program. The departure of my two classmates, who shared my language and teaching aspirations, left me feeling isolated and despondent, as we had always supported each other with homework and worked collaboratively as a team.

In 2011, I participated in my student teaching program under the guidance of an exceptional Spanish teacher named Sandra. She had graduated from MSMU five years prior and was volunteering as a master teacher. For three months, she would be my mentor. During this period, I was to shadow her in the classroom, acquiring the skills to teach Spanish. Sandra was a relaxed and approachable teacher, adored by her students, and the affection was mutual. I felt fortunate to be part of such a positive environment, where the warmth and camaraderie were palpable.

In 2012, I graduated from Saint Mary's with my teaching credential, and Henry was set to graduate from Channel Islands with his bachelor's degree. However, he dropped out, just two classes short of completing his degree. At that time, I was fifty six year old, and Henry was twenty two. Upon graduating from MSMC, I eagerly sought a teaching position in Spanish. While serving as a substitute teacher, I applied to various schools, but only one offered me a role.

This role, however, did not lead to actual teaching. As students and parents lodged complaints against me, the directors suggested I improve my rapport with the students to reduce parental complaints. Despite, my attempts, the students remained disinterested in my elective class for junior high students in Los Angeles, preferring to talk about baseball or soccer instead of concentrating on the lessons. During one incident, the principal was so upset by the disorder in my class that she intervened just as five students rushed to the restroom, flouting the one-at-a-time rule.

Their laughter and nonchalance led me to hand in my two weeks' notice. The principal, enraged, insisted on my immediate exit and forbade my return, opting to let go of a new teacher rather than confront the parents of the disruptive students. I accepted the position as a Spanish teacher at this school because I thought the principal knowing that it was my first year teaching was going to support me.

I also resigned because the commute from Valencia, California, to Los Angeles was unbearable. Moreover, they paid me only 100 dollars a day, which they claimed was the standard salary for substitute teachers in Los Angeles. However, they employed me as a Spanish teacher, not as a substitute. I went back working as a substitute for the Palmdale School District because I never resigned. It was OK in those days to have a long term subbing engagement with another district or leave the subbing position for a few months and return to be called as needed.

## Bringing Light to Elective Classes and Substitute Teachers

Elective classes are often viewed by students and parents as less essential than core subjects like English or Math. Teachers of music, foreign languages, art, and other electives sometimes lack support from school directors. In some places, resources are scarce, and schools may not offer these classes or delay hiring substitutes when a teacher vacates a position.

Substitute teachers are permitted to teach any subject and they are provided with a lesson plan upon arrival. They are expected to inform the students that their regular teacher prepared the lesson and to distribute the assigned pages or worksheets to keep them engaged. While some students adhere to the instructions, others are indifferent, perceiving the substitute as a transient figure who won't return.

As a substitute teacher for seven years, I became familiar with schools where the principal supported us and those where we worked just once and never returned. After a year, teachers began requesting me by name for subsequent substitute opportunities. I was fortunate to fill long-term positions, sometimes lasting a week or a month, assisting wonderful students.

During recess supervision, I conversed with other substitutes, sharing insights about favorable schools. The daily pay rate from different school districts was less important to us than finding students who showed respect and followed their regular teachers' instructions. Fellow substitutes shared their experiences, ranging from five to twelve years in the role. Despite my dedication, I harbored concerns about securing a permanent classroom of my own.

## Landing my Ideal Role as a Spanish Educator

In 2017, while I was working as a substitute teacher for the Palmdale School District, I got a call for an interview scheduled for the following day. After attending the interview, I was offered the job on the spot. The hiring institution was a charter school founded sixteen years ago by visionary educators who sought to bring innovative methods to teaching. Despite the school's sixteen years of operation, challenges were on the horizon.

Nevertheless, I spent a fantastic year teaching Spanish across various levels. I taught Spanish I to beginners, Spanish II to those who had completed the first level, and Spanish III to students requiring an advanced class. Additionally, I instructed students on the verge of graduation who, for some reason, needed Spanish IV. This was fine by me; I felt equipped to teach Spanish at the college level. While most students were delightful, a few youthful spirits presented challenges.

Fortunately, I had the unwavering support of the administration and my colleagues—experienced teachers with five to ten years at the school—who were always ready to assist me. My joy was immense when the school director informed me that I would be returning the next year as a Spanish teacher. The director awarded all the returning teachers with a bonus. When I opened my envelope and saw the check, I was astounded by the amount. It was enough to cover a trip to Spain, including hotel and airfare. For the first time ever, I was going to experience Spain.

In early August of 2018, the school director delivered the unfortunate news to us teachers. He had made multiple attempts to secure the necessary support to continue operating as a charter school in Palmdale. However, the Palmdale school district was no longer willing to assist. This left us teachers, the students, and the parents heartbroken and angry. There was a prevailing belief that the district desired to have all these students to them. The district loomed large like a giant, while the charter school seemed like a small entity with little chance of winning this struggle.

## How I Financed Writing my Memoir

I remember coming across an article in the June 17, 1991, edition titled "Christopher Columbus and Queen Isabella of Spain Consummate Their Relationship, Santa Fe, January, 1492," which made me wonder if it was factual or satirical. The story was compelling, featuring two historical icons. Growing up in Mexico, I was told of the noble Spanish queen who allegedly pawned her jewels to fund Columbus's epic voyage.

The distinction between reality and myth in these narratives can often become indistinct, yet history has a way of revealing the truth. Presently, I am in pursuit of financial support to pen my memoirs. At the pawn shop, I received an offer of $400 to pawn my jewels or $500 to sell it. I chose to sell, hoping to finance my book, complete it within a month, sell enough copies to afford new clothes, and perhaps repurchase the jewels —treasured gifts from my husband and daughter over the past fifty years—if the sales exceed my expectations.

Author's Note: The aforementioned tale was woven to add drama to my book. Funding the writing of memoirs is challenging, particularly with the slim chances of recovering the costs. As I strive to create a lasting legacy, I embrace the seemingly unattainable. This monumental step of faith in myself it's bolstered by an even stronger faith in humanity. History teaches us that Columbus, too, was once considered a madman, risking death and the ruin of his ships.

Yet, we know he was sane. We inhabit the land he unveiled. I wish to pay tribute to Columbus, the Queen of Spain, and their monumental gift to mankind. The jewels I received for my fifteenth birthday in 1971, I have sold. This book is my modest offering; the absence of the jewels does not trouble me. For this book is my new treasure, destined to outshine the most illustrious diamond for all time. God willing!

## This is the end of my Story

Life can be harsh, and there are times when we must pause, our education to care for our loved ones. I believe that God has granted me the inspiration to write as a solace for my suffering. Just as someone mentioned, one day, the Mexican singer Juan Gabriel created beautiful melodies from his pain, I am crafting lovely poems and stories to bring joy to women and children. I want to give you, my dear reader the following short stories and poems. Take these writings as a bonus for buying my memoir.

While reading them you will find more information about my pain and struggling to survive this cruel world alone while finishing raising my beautiful children. They kept me going, my schooling kept me going, and my job kept me going. Nowadays what's keep me going is the hope to be recognized as a domestic violence survivor. I hope that my self-published books will do the teaching now that I am home nursing my weak body going back to health. Please keep reading that I will continue writing for as long I have my computer and my wonderful books at my side.


Happy trails dear readers,

Sincerely,

Maria Morales
Teacher and Author

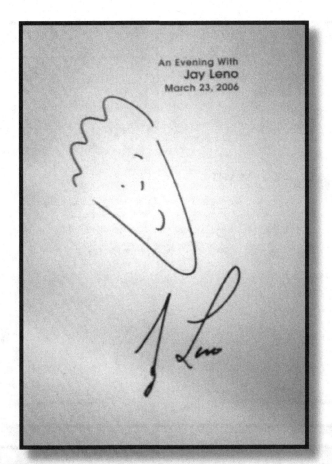

## State of Texas
## Certificate of High School Equivalency

is awarded to **MARIA MORALES**

who has demonstrated satisfactory performance
in the General Educational Development Testing Program
that meets standards prescribed by the Texas Education Agency.

JANUARY 29, 1990
Date

ENGLISH
Test Version

784425
Certificate Number

*W. Kirby*
Commissioner of Education

THE STATE OF TEXAS

---

Congratulations to

# Maria Morales

Upon completion of
Mount St. Mary's College
Secondary Teacher Preparation Program
Awarded at the Teacher Reception
May 4, 2011

*Carol Johnston*
Dr. Carol Johnston, Acting Program Director

*Shelly Tochluk*
Dr. Shelly Tochluk, Education Department Chair

**Los Angeles Times**

*Times Mirror Square*
*Los Angeles, CA 90053*
*213.237.5000*

*Thanks for sending the book
Maria — You're a very good
writer! And it's a nice
job of printing + an excellent
cover!*

*Sincerely, Al Martinez*

---

# CERTIFICATE OF CONGRESSIONAL RECOGNITION

PRESENTED TO

*Maria Morales*

**MEMBER**

IN RECOGNITION OF YOUR INVALUABLE LEADERSHIP AND CONTRIBUTION
TO THE BOARD OF THE SAMUEL DIXON FAMILY HEALTH CENTER

*July 22nd, 2019*

DATE

*Katie Hill*

KATIE HILL
MEMBER OF CONGRESS
25TH CONGRESSIONAL DISTRICT OF CALIFORNIA

## State Assembly

CERTIFICATE OF RECOGNITION

### Maria Morales

SAMUEL DIXON FAMILY HEALTH CENTERS

### BOARD MEMBER

*In honor of your distinguished service as a Board Member of Samuel Dixon Family Health Centers. I commend your commitment to the organization and their mission to promote quality healthcare. Thank you for your leadership and for sharing your expertise.*

Dante Acosta
ASSEMBLYMAN, 38TH DISTRICT

July 2018

---

*Attention: Teen Group*

*Guest Speaker*

## Maria Morales from Valencia High School

*Earn 15 points!*
*Thursday, March 15, 2007*
*6 p.m.*

*Start earning points for*
*This Summer Camp Trip!*

My México

A sacred land was given to the Aztecs by their Gods. This new home was going to be an enchanted place beside majestic volcanoes. The tears that México sheds these days could fill a brand new lake. A sacred place has been dishonored by criminal hands that kill women and children. Where can we find the Gods that helped the Aztecs? Our hope is dying while we witness such horrible massacres.

Popocatepetl

Iztaccihuatl

Words By
María Morales 2-2-11
"My México"
Illustration By
Richard Morales 3-20-11

She also included, the photos of her hands taking care of a bunch
of onions remembering her days working on the fields.

# Index for My Short Stories

# A Tale of a Mother and a Soldier

Our family resided in Santa Clarita, CA for three decades. During that time I was a proud mother and eventually achieved my goals of becoming a Spanish teacher, now retired. I fondly recall my oldest son, Trinidad Morales Jr., who at sixteen began working at Six Flags Magic Mountain theme park in Valencia, CA. His goals in life at the time were simple. They were to purchase video games and save for a car, all while balancing high school during the week and work on weekends. Trinidad, graduated in the year 2000, but chose not to attend his graduation, as he was not fond of parties.

He briefly attended community college, but left due to the challenges he faced, including the lack of a car and insufficient funds. His job at Magic Mountain ended, and he occasionally worked at a pizza place in Valencia. As a mother, I was overwhelmed by the terrible dilemma my son faced. While attending community college classes at night and working as a kindergarten teacher during the day, in August 2001, I took my two sons, aged 17 and 19, to an American Army recruiting center. I instructed them to gather information. Upon returning to pick them up, my son Trinidad declared he had enlisted by signing the contract, while his brother chose not to.

The month after, the horrific events of 9/11 unfolded. Overcome with shock, I turned to my son. He said, "I am a soldier, mother." At 42, ever since joining the army, he has never lacked for cars or money. The military taught him to drive. He has seen the world, in times of conflict and peace alike. One day, he recounted how his sergeant had barked at him, "Morales, pack your bags, you're off to Egypt, the Philippines, or Japan,". He never hesitated when ordered to be deployed to any nation that required his service. My son takes great pride in serving as a soldier for The United States of America. I am immensely proud of him and of my own career as a retired teacher from my homeland: The United States of America.

# A Lonely Mother

I accompanied my mother to visit her cousin's eldest daughter, Clare who was twenty years old and had recently given birth. In Latino culture, it's customary to visit the family to offer congratulations after a baby's birth. We found Clare alone at home with her newborn; she was not married and had the status of a mistress rather than a wife. Our visit was brief, lasting only a few minutes, which puzzled me considering the hour-long bus journey we had undertaken to reach her. I spoke very little during the visit; it was my mother who conversed mostly.

She was overjoyed to see the child, yet I could sense her anger towards Clare. The words they exchanged linger in my memory, not of joy, but of sorrow. "How can you live here alone? You deserve so much better," she said. Upon returning home, my mother finally addressed me, "We shall not visit her again. Our visit was solely for the baby. She is obstinate, unwilling to leave the married man. She made her choice, and now she must endure the consequences of living in solitude, forever without a spouse by her side."

At twenty, the same age as Clare, I was a student living under my mother's roof, unable to muster the courage to defy her and see Clare. My mother's wishes were absolute, unquestioned laws within our family. Now, I am left with countless questions, though it may be too late for Clare. I ponder whether Clare's predicament stemmed from love or fear. The man was fifty, a detective, a member of the police force, affluent and influential. In contrast, Clare's family was impoverished and intimidated.

Now, as a mother to five adult children, I comprehend my mother's perspective but empathize with Clare. I would never abandon my daughter to confront the world on her own. Raising a family is a monumental task that requires abundant support. When a mother is isolated and desolate, her children inevitably suffer, bearing those emotional scars indefinitely. Children often bear the brunt of their parents' errors, yet some mistakes are made out of love, fear, or a combination of both.

# A Fortunate Child

Today, I attended a college fair at San Fernando High School. I learned about the fair thanks to Elisa Cortez, the Director of Student Recruitment & School Relations at College of the Canyons. I brought my newspaper, anticipating some downtime to read. However, that was not the case! With Elisa's preparation, we were constantly engaged, addressing inquiries about furthering education for the students.

My enthusiasm was solely for C.O.C., but Elisa was also providing information on other institutions. She was there to present the students with options. She advised them to consider themselves as customers, to gather ample information, pose questions, and make educated decisions. I absorbed her advice and sought to emulate her approach. My goal is to continue attending college fairs, armed with my fervor for C.O.C. and the necessary knowledge to genuinely assist the students and their families.

Elisa invited me to lunch where we discussed my children. She confided in me her plans to adopt, revealing that she's attending parenting classes for adoption, aiming to adopt a child aged two to five. She's an extraordinary woman, ready to raise a child on her own. As a single woman determined to start her family, I believe she'll be an exceptional mother.

Her love for children is evident, and her career is dedicated to aiding other parents' children in pursuing education at C.O.C. or their chosen colleges. After lunch, we parted ways; she to her adoption classes, and I to tend to my young adults at home. They may not seek me out when they return, but I find joy in cooking for them. It seems a woman's nurturing instinct is everlasting.

# A Table for Seven

Twenty five years ago, when my family and I would go to a restaurant, we always asked for a table for seven. The waiter sometimes asked us to wait for a few minutes because they had to put together two small tables to accommodate my big family. We used to go to dinner every Sunday. Sometimes, we went to Marie Callender's, el Torito, or Sizzler.

Sometimes, we had to split the family up because my husband wanted to go to Red Lobster and I couldn't stand sea food. I used to drop him and the boys off at Red Lobster and take the girls with me to Marie Callender's in Valencia, California. We didn't fight with each other because the restaurant choice, we respected each other's preferences. My husband didn't care how much we spent eating out. He always said that the important thing was that we be happy. A lot happened in 25 years. My children grew into responsible adults, my husband and I divorced.

Last year, my children invited me to dinner for a New Year's Day. When the waiter asked for how many, to my surprise my oldest son said, "A table for seven, please." I couldn't believe that once again, we were asking for a table for seven. My youngest daughter husband and one family friend joined four of my five children and me for dinner. The dinner was wonderful!

# A Tale of Two Sisters

Last year, I had a phone conversation with my sister, whom I hadn't seen since 1989. I asked her age, and she replied that she was forty years old. In my mind, she would always be twenty. It was hard to believe she was only seven years younger than me. "How is that possible?" I asked. "I'm only seven years older than you, yet I took care of you." "You took care of all of us, Maria," she responded.

I often reflect on how I managed it. I was just a child myself, yet I took care of my younger siblings. Our mother was too busy with laundry work outside the home to tend to them, so I was in charge. I fed them, kept them out of trouble, and sang them to sleep. Now, my sister teaches English in Mexico, and I teach Spanish in California.

She worked as a nanny in California for two years, attending school in the evenings to learn English before returning to Mexico. My sister is among the few who declined the American dream, choosing instead to teach English back home. She educates the children of affluent families who visit California solely for vacations. Her students have no aspirations of living in America; they are already prosperous in Mexico.

Seeking advice for my classes, I turned to my sister. Now, she assists me with new teaching materials for my students who wish to learn Spanish for their vacations in Mexico. Ironically, while she teaches English in Mexico, I teach Spanish in California. The children of wealthy Mexicans will vacation in California, and American children will do the same in Mexico. This is the story of two sisters, two nations, and two languages, united by our passion for teaching and nurturing a new generation of students who may one day meet on the golden beaches of California.

# A Dreamer's Silent Prayer

At the age of five, Carlitos was faced with a harsh reality by his mother. "Tomorrow, you begin kindergarten, and there's something you must grasp," she explained. "Our birthplace is Mexico, but you have to tell everyone you were born in LA. We need to conceal the truth, or they'll send us back to a place where I can't provide you with an education or a decent life. My love for this country equals yours. After your father departed, an American family showed us kindness, and from that moment, America became our home."

Carlitos would recite the Pledge of Allegiance at school with such fervor that his teachers thought he was praying, not pledging. They were correct; with each recitation, he shut his eyes, wishing for a miracle to truly belong to this nation. Upon high school graduation with honors, his teachers encouraged him to attend college. He misled them, saying he would go to university and aspire to teach. His friends enlisted in the military post-graduation, and he realized their paths would likely never cross again.

His intention was to move to a different state and begin afresh. Months after graduation, Carlos' mother died, leaving him solitary in a country that didn't feel like his own. Now at thirty, Carlos is employed in construction, his mother's memory a constant companion. He continues to recite the Pledge of Allegiance, clinging to it as his daily prayer, awaiting a long-delayed miracle to materialize.

# Anger and Bitterness

As I watched a movie on TV, a character uttered, "Anger and bitterness are part of one's narrative." I was startled—it seemed as if they were addressing me, proclaiming, "Anger and bitterness define you!" My anger is not solely self-directed; it encompasses the whole world, a world that frequently lets down women. In this world, it is a tragic reality that some women perish by their spouses' hands.

I rescued myself. To reiterate: my survival is due to my escape, despite his multiple attempts on my life. Like a contemporary Scheherazade, I crafted a story that he accepted as truth. My resolve is to recount my story until we see a transformation—until women are protected as though they are the Eighth Wonder of the World.

I contemplate: What would become of this world if women ceased to exist?

An answer would be greatly valued.

# Art in the Home

This is the story of Jennifer, a young girl with a love for sweeping the patio. In her large family of eight girls and four boys; everyone contributed to the housework, animal care, and managing their small plot of land during difficult economic times. Jennifer's family discouraged her from sweeping, believing she was too small for the task. She never went to school, in those days the early 1900 hundreds, schools were rare.

Instead, Jennifer was assigned the daily task of making tortillas. She spent her days in the kitchen, diligently preparing tortillas for her family. Without any complaints, she accepted that sometimes tortillas were their only meal. She made each tortilla with happiness, singing songs of her homeland while she worked. She had learned the songs listening to her mother. While the mother sang to the babies, she was listening!

Her singing might not have been professionally trained, but it carried the depth of her humble, generous spirit. On one occasion, while sweeping, Jennifer was seen embellishing the patio with paintings of birds and ducklings. Her parents, who valued chores over artistic expression, dissuaded her from this activity. Consequently, the art world missed out on a potential painter, while the culinary world gained a dedicated cook.

# An Audience

Al Martinez penned his biweekly column today. I never miss it because he writes with such sincerity. Today's piece was particularly poignant, discussing the melancholy of having no audience to share his book with. He touched on the loneliness an author can feel when left alone, without anyone to appreciate their work. Just yesterday, a friend mentioned that one of her acquaintances plans to purchase two copies of my book. Hearing that was like a symphony to my ears; two copies signify that someone values my work enough to buy it.

To me, this minor update is a major milestone. Imagining someone reading my book and wanting to share it with a friend to the extent of buying two copies is incredibly thrilling. I empathize with Al Martinez's sadness; his book deserves a spot on the bestseller list. He has a gift for writing and reaching out to the lonely heart, yet it seems today's society overlooks the matters of the heart.

Why read a book when the movie "The Da Vinci Code" premieres today and everyone is eager to watch it?

Book enthusiasts may seem like dinosaurs nearing extinction, but we persist. I know this because someone is purchasing two copies of my book. I know this because I am buying Al Martinez's book. Al Martinez, you have an audience; I eagerly await your columns every Monday and Friday. Don't feel downhearted; you're not alone. Movies may come and go, but books are eternal. This generation might not cherish books, but perhaps the next one will.

# Aurora's Family

What constitutes a family? In modern times, the traditional definition of a family remains largely unchanged: a family typically includes a father, a mother, and their children. However, nowadays, it's common for families to include aunts, uncles, and grandparents who play parental roles for the younger generation.

When a parent is unable to care for their family, another relative often steps in as the caretaker. Such is the case for Aurora and her seven children: three are her own, three are her late sister's, and one is a nephew from another sister who is a "free spirit." Aurora embraces the responsibility of caring for all seven children, finding their love to be her greatest reward.

As I tutor her two eldest children, I witness the unique structure of their family and Aurora's dedication and love for her large family, despite the challenging circumstances of its formation. While tutoring at the dining room table, I see Aurora at the kitchen table, assisting the two youngest with homework. Her gentle yet firm voice directs the others to shower or walk the family pet. She commands like a sergeant, and they obey like soldiers, knowing she is their steadfast support through tough times. Aurora accompanies the children to school recitals, boys and girls clubs, and university tours.

Her two eldest are preparing to leave for college this summer, starting new chapters of their lives. Aurora manages a home brimming with children and joy, the painful memories of her divorce and the loss of her sister and brother-in-law fading amidst the creation of new memories with her expanded family. While some may fear the future, Aurora greets it with open arms, confident in the knowledge that she is not alone, with seven family members by her side.

# Bare Walls

The walls were bare, not from a recent move, but due to the family's poverty that precluded buying pictures. As time passed, ten children arrived one after another—seven girls and three boys. Among them, two girls attended school, as did the youngest boy. Today, if you visit the old house, it's unrecognizable.

The daughters added rooms and adorned the walls with pictures, while the sons painted the exterior, cultivated fruit trees, and planted vibrant flowers. The elderly couple now spends time on their porch, reminiscing about their children. This family, once poor in possessions, is now rich in love and care—a wealth their children, who remember their humble beginnings, will forever cherish.

# Blooming Flowers

"Not all flowers bloom at the same time." This adage resonates deeply with the diversity lessons from my Sociology 101 class. Understanding the varied backgrounds of the students we will one day teach is crucial. America isn't merely a single group leading society; it's a "Melting Pot" brimming with individuals who contribute their unique talents and dreams to this era.

Indeed, these are promising times; trailblazers like Martin Luther King and Cesar Chavez have opened doors. It's our duty to keep these doors ajar so that every student can access the gift of education and a chance at a better life. We ought to assist our students by providing guidance, resources, and unwavering support to help them reach their educational aspirations.

Certainly, these are demanding times for teachers and educators. Their role is essential not just in teaching but also in mentoring the students. Mentorship holds immense value, especially for those students lacking a role model. In the absence of role models, many students might struggle to attain an education. Let us hope that all our flowers will bloom, and we can delight in the splendor of their blossoming.

# Broken Rules

Among all the rules I've broken to get to where I am today, which one do I regret the most, or which am I glad I broke? Love wasn't part of my aspirations; I was sexually abused at six, leaving me forever scarred. I harbored a fear of men. Don't label me a liar; I lied to survive, and it's because of those lies— I'm alive.

My name is Maria Morales, and I am sixty-eight years old. I was born in Mexico in 1956, the third of ten children, with three boys and seven girls. As the eldest girl, I always followed my dad wherever he went. Every other month, he would take my two older brothers and me to the barbershop—the boys for haircuts, and me to read comic books. At ten years old, I adored reading. Back then, Mexico had no public libraries, so my father would buy the newspaper daily and comic books twice a week.

I was always the second to read the paper after my father. Reading was more than a hobby for me; it was a necessity. The barber, upon finishing with the boys, would invariably ask if I needed a haircut, too. My response was consistently affirmative: Yes! Monterrey, my hometown, has a desert-like climate, scorching in the summer. I reveled in the sensation of the air on my neck and face. Some kids teased me, saying I looked like a boy, but my older brothers were always there, shielding me from the neighborhood bullies.

Attending church on Sunday mornings was a cherished ritual for me, as it was a time to learn prayers and hymns. Singing alongside my siblings brought me joy. At home, the routine was constant: cleaning, caring for my younger siblings, and hoping they would sleep early so I could indulge in reading. My mother disapproved; she would confiscate my newspaper out of envy. Illiterate, she viewed my reading as a waste of time that could be spent on chores.

Despite her harshness, I stood my ground, threatening to inform my father, which led her to relent. However, this came after a severe scolding. My father, perpetually occupied with his job at the steel factory, was under the impression that everything at home was fine, safely overseen by my mother. As time passed and disputes became frequent, she came to understand the need to give me space. I assumed the role of aiding my siblings with their schoolwork, handling the shopping, and soothing the little ones to sleep.

I started working at a sewing factory, enduring shifts from eight in the morning to six, depending on city buses that were always old, dirty, and delayed. After half a decade at a sewing factory, the time has come for me to depart and seek new ways to support my family. In Mexico, I never had a boyfriend; my love for reading sustained me, and I never imagined writing about my life. I lived in poverty, just another factory worker among thousands. Leaving Mexico wasn't difficult, but parting from my sisters felt like my heart was being torn out. I was there when my mother returned home from the hospital. I sang them beautiful songs and helped them pen their first letters. They called me sister, but my love for them was almost maternal.

# Centro Cultural Lumen- my High School

In my country, I had the good fortune of attending school foe eleven years. I completed high school, but my aspiration to attend college dissipated. My education journey through primary and secondary school was typical, involving school attendance, assisting with household chores, and completing homework. However, as high school approached, I faced the harsh reality that it was unattainable. My family simply couldn't afford the textbooks required.

The prospect of not continuing my education felt like the end of the world; it was akin to knowing hell! For two years, I stayed home, aiding my younger sisters with their studies. By assisting them, I absorbed their textbooks, memorizing lessons and poems. Daily newspaper reading became a beacon of light for my tormented soul. At 18, I began working at a sewing factory. For two years, my life oscillated between work and home, but my heart remained aching to the idea of not pursuing higher education.

One day, while strolling down a street, I spotted a sign for "Lumen Cultural Center," a private high school for women only. Driven by curiosity, I stepped inside to learn more. They described it as a private high school tailored for young women who worked daytime jobs, but were seeking evening education. Classes were scheduled from 6:30 PM to 9:30 PM. Compelled, I signed up immediately. When I announced this at home, skepticism greeted me. "You're crazy," my family exclaimed.

"How will you balance work and study?" Nevertheless, I seized the chance before me. Going to school was not a chore; it was like grasping at the stars. For two years, my daily schedule was a non-stop cycle: work from 8 AM to 6 PM, then off to school, using the bus ride to finish my homework. At 22, I completed high school. While my friends eagerly prepared for graduation, I faced the reality that my college aspirations remained just dreams.

With my younger sisters in school, our finances stretched too thin to include my higher education. A profound sadness filled me as my dreams were curtailed once more. However, the school principal, aware of my situation, encouraged me to attend the prom and generously provided fabric for a dress.

"Maria," she insisted, "you deserve to experience the prom; you've earned it."

Grateful, I returned home and decided to have dresses made for my little sisters from the fabric. "They'll look beautiful in new dresses," remarked my sister. I kept the origin of the material a secret, protecting her from a painful truth. My graduation passed without celebration; the prospect of not attending college felt like a betrayal of my aspirations. To me, it was akin to a life sentence without education.

Yet, my heart found solace abroad, in a country that welcomed me and offered the education I yearned for. This year marked my College of the Canyons graduation, which equates to two years of college in my homeland. Only two more years remain until I earn my college degree—a minor wait after a thirty-year longing. My affection for this nation, for the opportunities it has granted me, knows no bounds.

I extend an invitation to all who value education to embrace schooling, for it is indeed a privilege. Some may label my persistent pursuit of knowledge as madness, but it is a divine madness that fuels my love for my education, my new home, and the life I've begun anew. Many have considered me intelligent for mastering English as an adult while maintaining a daytime job.

I often say that my stubbornness rivals that of a mule, and doing my homework never felt like punishment, but rather a labor of love, as learning is akin to drinking from a blessed fountain.

# Crazy for Getting an Education

One day, so cloudy and sad, my mother, and I were waiting for the city bus that would take us to our house. When the bus passed by the university, I told my mother: "One day, I am going to study at this university." My mother looked at me and said: "You are crazy, we are poor." My mother wasn't wrong, I was crazy about an education and we were really poor. Thanks to my two older brothers, my sister Luisa, and me, the younger siblings were able to go to college.

The elder siblings have consistently provided financial and moral support to forge a path forward. The sacrifices of my two brothers have allowed their siblings to seek education and establish professional careers. I am endlessly grateful to my two older brothers, and I encourage anyone with an elder sibling who has helped a family member attend college to take a moment to express their thanks!

I'm sharing, the professions that the Pérez family achieved: Maria, 68, and Lisa, 61, are teachers. Luisa, 65, and Catalina, 56, serve as secretaries. Susana, 63, and Marina, 58, are in the medical field, while Jose Alberto, 53, is an engineer. For me, it took nearly two decades to graduate as a teacher. Financial constraints prevented me from attending college in Mexico, and in California, my husband's refusal was the barrier.

However, once we parted ways, the confines of what I called home were no longer a restraint, and I pursued college education. I often recount my journey to inspire students who encounter difficulties in pursuing higher education. Trust me, navigating life without a college degree is challenging. Embrace the college experience, earn your degree, and find happiness—much like I did!

# Cooking for my Son

I often ponder whether my culinary traditions will perish with me. My son adores the dishes I prepare, yet he lacks the knowledge to recreate them. Just yesterday, I was preparing *chiles rellenos* (pasilla peppers), a dish deeply rooted in Mexican tradition. The process takes two hours, but the result justifies the effort. The chiles rellenos served in restaurants are different; they bear the name but lack the authenticity. Our recipe, passed down from my grandmother to my mother, has been preserved not through written words, as they were illiterate, but etched in their hearts.

I believe that cooking this dish requires heart, given its demanding nature. I've shared with my son that I never made *chiles rellenos* while in Mexico; it was my mother who crafted them. She never explicitly taught me; instead, I learned by observing her roast the peppers, clean them, and stuff them with a savory blend of meat, potatoes, and fresh cheese. Only one of my children relishes *chiles rellenos*, and it's imperative he learns to prepare them. It's a labor of love, a heritage from the Indians to the mestizos, a labor my son must embrace to ensure our culinary legacy endures for his children, even after I'm gone.

# Cheaper by the Dozen, the Book

I've watched the movie "Cheaper by the Dozen" a couple of times, and my children adore it. While the film is humorous, it pales in comparison to the book. I stumbled upon the book at a public library sale where they were clearing out old stock. The clerk charged me ten cents for it, which made me ponder the stark contrast in price between watching the film and purchasing the book.

Upon reading, I couldn't help but contrast it with its cinematic counterpart. The film leaves you cheerful, whereas the book blends happiness with sorrow, weaving tales of a large family. The father is depicted as both authoritarian and noble. Caroline, a dear friend, found the father's temperament too reminiscent of her own father's to continue reading, despite my assurance of his kindness. Another friend declined to read the book, believing it would be redundant to the film, not realizing the stark differences.

The book celebrates a loving family's unity and resilience, especially after the father's passing when the mother steps up to sustain the family bond. For me, the crux is the importance of family unity. While laughter and relaxation are necessary, it's also crucial to grasp the deeper message of "Cheaper by the Dozen." My philosophy teacher, forty years ago, taught me that the book is always better than the movie. My philosophy teacher was right, the book is always better!

# Change

Change is beneficial. We experience seasons that reveal the beauty of a transforming .world. From the chilly winter to the balmy days of spring, we embrace change. Yet, there's another kind of change: aging and the gradual loss of independence. With mixed feelings, I visited the senior citizen apartment complex, contemplating if I was ready for this move. After enduring noisy neighbors for too long, I made the decision to relocate.

Upon entering the building to obtain a rental application, I encountered an elderly man in a wheelchair by the door. I offered to assist him, but he declined, saying, "I don't need help with the door; I'm staying here because I'm just killing time." I thought about telling him that we're all in essence killing time, yet hoping for more days to live. I remained silent, though, and proceeded to the office.

The secretary handed me the application, and I returned home to complete it and begin packing. Once, I had a large house with a spacious yard and four cars in the garage. Now, the house is sold, my children have moved out, and my husband left me for a younger woman. Next month, I'll move into a one-bedroom apartment with a patio that fits a small table and two chairs.

I'm confronting this change with bravery and resolve. As long as I can work and care for my students, I'll be fine. My apartment will be a place to read, dine, and rest. My students, who keep me engaged and spirited, express gratitude for my assistance. I wish I could tell them they are the ones sustaining my sanity and life, but I refrain, not wanting to alarm them.

# Cheap Date

If you want a cheap date, Facebook me because, I don't have an iPod or smart phone.
Don't expect a fancy restaurant with a table cloth and wine glasses.
I can offer you only the dollar menu from Mc Donald's or Jack in the Box.
After dinner I will take you for a walk in the park, or the beach.
After our walk, I will take you to watch a movie.
Don't expect El Capitan or Edwards Cinema.
We can get a movie from the Red Box, and I will make homemade popcorn.
I hope you have a car, if not; we will take the city bus. I know my way around;
I promise you that it will only take us an hour or two from one place to the other.

Do you know any takers?

Signed by desperate and with no luck from Los Angeles, California.

# Compassion for a Lonely Mother

Last week, my daughter's best friend was given a baby shower. The party was held at a pizza restaurant and the two families got together to celebrate. I have known my daughter's friend since she was 12 years old. I wanted to share her family's happiness because this is their first grandchild. They not only invited relatives, but a great number of friends, neighbors and co- workers. She was beaming with happiness opening the presents and thanking all her loved ones for being there.

The following week I read about a young woman who was charged with murder for leaving her newborn son in a trash bin. I couldn't avoid comparing the two situations. In one hand we have a young girl celebrating life with her family and friends and in another we have a young woman giving birth alone. "What was she thinking?" That was my first reaction. Why didn't her maternal instincts kick in? Why didn't she ask for help?

I have a young daughter and many times I have warned her to be careful and not get pregnant. But I know that if she gets pregnant I will be there to help her. Why should we blame this young girl for leaving her baby in the trash bin? We were not there when she found out that she was pregnant. We were not there when she was hoping that her situation would just go back to normal, so she could keep going to school.

My mother gave birth to ten children and I don't remember any maternal instincts from her. She used to go outside to do the laundry and I was the one taking care of "her children." I took care of all my children not having a good role model. We need to have compassion for this young girl; we have to be in her shoes to cast any stones. I do cry for the baby that died. I also cry for the young woman whose life has been changed forever.

We do have programs to help pregnant women, one of them is called "Without Questions" In this program, you can live your baby at any fire station after the baby is born and you just can go on with your life. But sadly some people like this young woman still will do the unthinkable and leave her newborn in a trash bin. Not everybody is as lucky as my daughter's friend. Some people hardly can take care of themselves let alone take care of a baby. Some are scared, some are left alone to take a life and death decision in their hands. And sadly they make the wrong decision.

# Donating Blood

I entered the Red Cross office to donate blood. The nurse inquired about my weight, and I responded: 105 lbs. It was 1980, a year after my arrival from Mexico to California. I was informed that the minimum weight for donation was 110 lbs and was thanked for my visit. Leaving the office, it took a decade before I began donating blood, now at 140 lbs. Amidst raising a family, attending school, and working, I found time for this cause. Lacking funds to contribute financially, donating blood boosted my self-esteem. The knowledge that my donation could save lives post-surgery or accidents was immensely rewarding.

The exact number of times I've donated is unclear, perhaps 35 to 40. The Red Cross occasionally contacts me to remind me it's time to donate again. They have become friends who have my number. I won't sugarcoat it; donating blood is a demanding and sometimes painful task. Visits to the Red Cross can last one to two hours. Occasionally, nurses struggle to locate a vein, persisting until blood flows into the collection bag. Afterward, there's a wait of 10 to 15 minutes before you can hydrate with a drink and enjoy a snack, which I sometimes take for the road. The next day, a blue mark on my arm serves as a proud reminder of the life saved by my donation. I plan to return in 3 to 4 months, continuing to donate as long as I'm called upon to help save lives.

# Dolores Huerta

Having Dolores Huerta as the commencement speaker at my graduation from California State University, Bakersfield was a profound honor. This formidable woman will undoubtedly be recognized in history books for her commitment to enhancing the living conditions of farm workers. As the president of The Dolores Huerta Foundation, she leads a non-profit organization dedicated to creating active communities that advocate for equitable access to health care, housing, education, employment, civic engagement, and economic resources, particularly for women and youth.

Hearing Huerta speak felt like a summons to serve the community. As newly minted professionals, we are called upon to dedicate our lives to improving the conditions of those in need. We must heed Mrs. Huerta's call to better our community and create a more equitable world for all. Currently known as a Labor leader, she will, in time, be celebrated as a Peace leader, for her struggle is for justice, and justice is the foundation of peace. My deepest gratitude goes to Dolores Huerta for her inspiring words. I will forever cherish the memory of her addressing my graduation. I aspire to one day share with my grandchildren that I was fortunate enough to be inspired by the great Dolores Huerta.

# Dinner

It was 7:00 PM, and I was on my way to meet a friend for dinner. A nice meal after a long day's work is a time to unwind and discuss our families. As we began our meal inside the restaurant, I noticed an old building across the street undergoing renovations. Workers were hoisting heavy wooden beams. Watching them, I couldn't help but wonder, "When will they have their dinner?" They were still laboring, even past seven. My friend redirected my attention to our conversation.

It had been a month since we last met, and there was much to catch up on. When she excused herself to the restroom, my gaze returned to the workers. By 8:00 PM, they were stowing their tools away. Relieved, I thought, "They're heading home to their families, to relax and enjoy a nice dinner, just like me." Yet, I pondered, how many have families waiting? How many return to an empty house with no meal prepared?

How many yearn for rest to brace for another grueling day of labor? Last week, we observed Labor Day, a holiday to honor workers enduring tough conditions. But the workers across the street deserve more than a holiday; they merit recognition for their sacrifices as construction workers. They persist until the task is complete, not ceasing at 5:00 PM to return to their families. Their workday spans from dawn till dusk.

# Empty Bottles of Perfume

On Friday, I visited Macy's to purchase my favorite perfume, Youth Dew by Estee Lauder. Although I still have a few new bottles, I couldn't resist their special offer. Estee Lauder occasionally runs a promotion where they give away a tote bag filled with cosmetics. I took advantage of this week's promotion, keeping the perfume for myself and distributing the tote bags and some cosmetics to my friends. I discovered this perfume twenty years ago while cleaning houses. One of my duties was to clean the perfume tray, and upon trying Youth Dew, I was captivated by its fragrance.

Occasionally, I would find empty bottles in the trash, which I cleaned and brought home. My daughters amassed a collection of these bottles, often pretending to sell perfumes or to be movie stars. I've adored this perfume for years and began purchasing it for myself a decade ago. Wearing it daily uplifts me, and I don't let memories of house cleaning overshadow my present.

Recently, a schoolyard supervisor offered me a ride on a rainy day. As I hopped into his golf cart, he remarked that I smelled like his mother and correctly guessed the perfume I was wearing. We shared a moment of connection over the scent and the common practice of buying it for the complimentary gifts. It was heartwarming to meet someone else familiar with Youth Dew. I'll continue wearing it, not just for the gifts, but also for the joy of sharing them with those I care about.

My eldest daughter occasionally chides me for my spending habits, frequently advising me to "save for a rainy day." I reassure her that I don't fret over rainy days because she's my umbrella. As the family's accountant and the one savvy with finances, she's the ideal candidate to invest in Estee Lauder stock. She went into accountant because she didn't know what to choose as a career. She was good at math, science, history, and all the subjects. I told her to become a teacher, like me. I don't won't to offend you mom," she said, but there is no money into teaching.

She chose accountant because it was a safe career. She's aware of my penchant for perfume; spotting a promotion in the newspaper is enough to tempt me into purchasing another bottle, despite having several unopened ones at home. Moreover, when a birthday approaches, there's no need for me to shop for gifts—I have a surplus of perfume bottles ready to be given. My daughters are well aware of this stash, and whenever they're headed to a birthday party without a gift, they turn to me for assistance. I'm always happy to share with them!.

# Food the New Poison

I offered her some cookies, saying, "Just take one or two." "You don't understand, Mom," she replied. "Would you offer a beer to an alcoholic?" I was speechless, so I just hugged her, and then she left. My relationship with my youngest daughter is quite strained. I'm afraid to speak to her and risk upsetting her, terrified that she might cut off communication with me. She has battled with her weight since childhood. Last year, she shed 100 pounds and aims to lose another 25 by her birthday next month.

I find it difficult to grasp her weight concerns, as I've never faced them myself. Growing up in a large, impoverished family in Mexico, we always shared our meals. I'm accustomed to cooking for many, yet I don't consume much. I save and eat modest portions daily, a habit from my days in Mexico. I don't need to share with siblings now, but I can still resist food, even when it's tempting. I'm aware that my food will be there tomorrow, waiting in the fridge, and I'll eat a bit then save the rest for later. Some people must carefully monitor their caloric intake.

Fast food has become the new poison, with its abundance and the constant food advertisements on TV urging us to indulge. My reading habit is intense—I must read daily—but it doesn't compromise my health. However, my daughter's weight issues are detrimental to her well-being. She attempted diets and exercise, but eventually realized her problem was too great to handle alone and sought medical assistance. My role is to support her efforts without judgment. I wish her all the strength she needs to overcome this illness.

This illness claimed the lives of Karen Carpenter, Tracy Gold, and many other gifted women who succumbed to the overwhelming voices of guilt and fear, leaving us to ponder.

# Founding a Good Book

Fern Michaels is a well known writer. I had read many of her books. I read her book, No Safe Secret, and I wasn't going to read the message to readers because I never do it. This book however left me with many questions, maybe reading the message to readers, I could find some answers. These are only few sentences of her powerful message, "I cannot know this for certain, but I think all of you out there know someone who has been sexually abused. I know I have. Way too many actually! The truth is, one person is too many."

Her message left me numb, cold, and sad. I am a sixty- eight old woman, and I was abused when I was six years old. The molester was my neighbor; he used to invite me to his house to play with balloons. He molested me while pretending to be my friend. I never told my family, I was afraid of him! We moved away from him few months later and I tried to forget this terrible incident, but I knew that I was not going to be able to date or marry because I was damaged for life!

# Forever Fifty

While some people yearn to turn back time and be twenty or thirty again, I believe life begins at fifty. Initially, the prospect of turning fifty filled me with dread. For months, I tried to ignore the impending arrival of my fiftieth birthday. Then it dawned on me that my youngest son would turn eighteen around the same time I reached fifty. Over the past fifty years, I've learned so much. I've raised five children, earned a degree from College of the Canyons, and started taking classes at Bakersfield University.

Thirty years ago, I was terrified of what lay ahead. I contemplated becoming a nun, seeking refuge in a convent, dedicating my life to God and the children in my care, and longing for someone to look after me, not realizing I was capable of self-care. The past fifty years have taught me that I can take care of myself, my family, and even children who aren't my own. My approach to life has changed; I now view life as a friend and no longer fear the future.

Each new day fills me with joy as I witness my children's accomplishments. I start my day with a cup of coffee in one hand and the newspaper in the other, and my day concludes at midnight after watching Jay Leno. Why Leno? Because I enjoy ending my day with laughter and Leno has a knack for that. After turning off the TV, I say a prayer for my children and all the children around the world. I rest, confident in the arrival of a new day—a day I will greet with the wisdom and serenity that being fifty years old brings. My wish is to be forever fifty!

# Honoring my Wonderful Aunt Maria

I first met Aunt Maria when I was nine years old; she visited our home to celebrate my First Holy Communion. Accompanying her were my grandmother and cousin Hilda. At fifteen, Hilda was an orphan, also residing in Guanajuato with my grandmother. Aunt Maria, childless and generous, welcomed Hilda into her home. However, at seventeen, Hilda eloped with her boyfriend. Subsequently, Aunt Maria requested my father's permission for my brother Andres to assist her in her small store.

My father consented, and Andres dedicated nearly three years to helping her. Additionally, Aunt Maria took in three more of our cousins after another uncle's wife passed away. With no children of her own, my aunt willingly accepted the children who were brought from Guanajuato. She was a remarkable woman, always eager to lend a hand to everyone. Tragically, Aunt Maria passed away six months after the children came to live with her, a loss that devastated my father, brother, and the entire family.

It was a profound sorrow to lose her. I was thirteen at the time, and it marked the first funeral I ever attended. My uncle from Guanajuato arrived to collect his children and sought my father's assistance in caring for them. Although my father sympathized with him, he was unable to aid his brother. With a large family of his own, he simply couldn't accommodate any more children. Sadly, we never saw my uncle or my little cousins again.

# He was Never my Lover

It is said that first love is never forgotten. I would like to forget, not only the first love, but also the second, the third and so many others that have passed through my life. Today I want to remember a love that could have been and was not. I met him at school, we talked on the phone for a while, but he never declared his love. One night, my boyfriend and I went out dancing at the San Fernando Palace in California. He went to get some beers and I sat at the table waiting for him. Then, Merejo, arrived and asked me to dance.

My boyfriend approached him and yelled: "Don't you want to dance with me, you bastard?" I was paralyzed, not knowing what to do. Merejo, said goodbye politely and left. My boyfriend, furious, kicked me out of the place. That man, my boyfriend, would become my husband and father of my five children. He did not allow me to go to parties or to birthdays of relatives or friends. One day, I asked him for a big favor: to let me attend my cousin Carmen's wedding. I would take all the children and we would just attend the ceremony at the church.

When I arrived, I saw him standing with his family. I approached him with my five children and we sat down. There he was, in front of me! During the moment of giving the peace, I wanted to say to him: "Save me from the monster that is my husband," but I couldn't. My eldest daughter was next to me and I was afraid that she might hear me and then tell her father. So we just exchanged a peace sign.

He gave me one too, and I never knew if he recognized me or remembered me. I saw him again, but fate seemed determined to prevent our communication. This time, we were in a restaurant, my youngest daughter and I, waiting for our food. Even though she was 20 years old, I was embarrassed to try to talk to him, especially since he was with someone. It's been 45 years since that day at school.

# Helida the new Math Teacher

What would you do if your child came home one day asking for help with their math homework? Some might call a tutor, others might admit math isn't their strong suit and leave the child to their own devices. Helida encountered this dilemma a decade ago. She felt ashamed to admit to her son that she couldn't assist with math because she had forgotten it. Despite working full-time, she made time to meet with his math teacher, expressing her desire to learn math to support her son. She also feared her son discovering her knowledge gap.

The teacher devised a plan: Helida would attend as a student under the guise of a parent volunteer, ensuring she volunteered during a different period than her son to avoid crossing paths. Her love for her son drove her to these lengths, but then something changed. The teacher's method of explaining math captivated Helida, and soon she found herself tutoring math to children. Now capable of aiding her son and others, the math teacher offered her a job. When Helida's employer relocated out of state, she chose to stay in California, close to her family.

She enrolled at CSUB, graduated last year, completed her teaching credentials this year, and is set to begin her master's degree at CSUN this fall. This brave parent exemplifies determination, not allowing her initial lack of knowledge to impede her son's education. She pursued schooling to master math and is now advancing to a master's degree. Helida, my tutor at CSUB, assisted me with a challenging math class I was close to failing, nearly causing me to abandon my own education.

# Honoring my two Big Terrific Brothers

In my household, the phrase "We don't have any money!" was frequently heard. Our family consisted of four children and our parents, residing in a modest home in the Hidalgo colony of Monterrey, Nuevo León, Mexico. My elder brothers, Andrés and Gil, were born in San Luis Potosí, Mexico, and Texas, USA, respectively. During that period, my father had journeyed to Texas to work as a "Bracero." The Bracero Program was an initiative established by the American and Mexican governments, benefiting both nations. It started in 1942 and concluded in 1964. My parents were among the multitudes of farm workers who benefited from this program.

However, my mother was deported to Tamaulipas shortly before I was born, and my father returned to Mexico to reunite with his family soon after my birth. My parents never returned to Texas; instead, they settled in Monterrey, a burgeoning city, with their three children born in various places. Andrés began working at 14 in my Aunt Maria's small grocery store and, after her death, joined my father in the factory at 17. Gil went back to Texas at 15, not to study, but to work. My brothers didn't attend secondary school due to the lack of funds for books. They harbored no resentment, understanding that the household's finances were prioritized for food and rent.

My two older brothers always supported our parents financially, addressing the family's numerous needs. They emulated our father: lifelong laborers, unable to pursue high school education. Thanks to them, the phrase "No Hay dinero" (we don't have any money) was unfamiliar to the younger siblings, who enjoyed candies, toys, and the privilege of having food, shelter, and secondary education. I was the first in my family to complete middle and high school, graduating in 1978 while working at a sewing factory in the mornings and attending a private night school.

Years later, in 2012, I achieved my goal of becoming a teacher in California. In this writing, I express my gratitude to my brothers, Andrés, 71, and Gil, 70. I often remind my students that education is for life. My brothers bestowed upon me this beautiful gift of education. Thanks to this gift, I could assist my children with their studies, preventing them from dropping out of school. This gift also empowered me to be self-reliant after my divorce in 2000. The Perez siblings have thrived professionally, largely due to Andrés and Gil. My elder brothers started working at fourteen to support our family. They didn't keep their earnings; instead, they contributed it to my father for food and school supplies. Both completed only up to the sixth grade.

Subsequently, they took up jobs, got married—one at 26, the other at 28—and raised wonderful families. My brother Gil passed away last year while awaiting heart surgery. Gil left California in 1991 for Texas, and I never saw him again. Unfortunately, I couldn't attend his funeral as I didn't have the funds. My two brother's sacrifices enabled their siblings to pursue an education and become professionals. Maria, 68, and Lisa, 61, are teachers. Luisa, 65, and Catalina, 56, serve as secretaries. Susana, 63, and Marina, 58, are in the medical field, while Jose Alberto, 53, is an engineer. Many of my sisters and I have independently led our families.

# Home

Recently, I was listening to "God Bless America" and couldn't help but reflect on the numerous times I've heard this moving song. To me, it's akin to a prayer, echoing through churches, my children's schools, and our home. English, being my second language, fills me with pride when I sing this song, as it signifies not only my grasp of the language but also my adoption of this culture. Gregory Maguire, in an essay for The Los Angeles Times, discusses teaching his three adopted children from various countries a language that will unite both his family and his nation.

He states, "Having a common language is the beginning of civilization, and civilizing our children is our best chance at preserving it." As a parent, Gregory dedicates time and effort to impart a language that will unlock countless opportunities for his children. I have done the same; English is the sole language spoken in our home. Home is a sanctuary to return to after life's journeys. As my children move forward with their lives, they know that upon their return, they will find their mother immersed in the same songs we once sang together in church, at school, and within the comfort of our home.

# I am the one Weaving Stories

Life unfolds as a narrative from the moment we enter the world. Some of us narrate it; others simply listen. Some harbor their tales deep within for an eternity, until the inevitable moment arrives for the story to be unveiled. I have learned to listen with my heart, and thus, my friends entrusted me with their narratives. I embraced their tales as my own, penned them down, and now, I return them to you.

Cherish these stories, for they hold more value than gold; gold may be pilfered, but stories remain untouched by thieves. Only the sagacious will continually seek a trustworthy and beloved confidant. Only they will preserve the stories, passing them on, allowing them to soar. A heartfelt story concludes with joy; I am beyond joy writing my own memoir and narrating wonderful stories. Believe me, I will reminisce your story and through it, narrate my own.

Life can be tough, and sometimes we need to put our education on hold to look after our loved ones. I feel that God has blessed me with the gift of writing as a comfort during my trials. In the same way that the Mexican singer Juan Gabriel composed beautiful melodies from his sorrow, I too am creating delightful poems and stories to bring happiness to women and children.

# I Left Him and Never Look Back

<hr/>

In June 1999, my husband was arrested by Emigration. He was detained for seven months in Los Angeles, and then, he was deported to Mexico. My family and I went to see him several times in Tijuana. Tijuana was the city where my husband was deported. He asked me to stay in Tijuana with him. I had been living for 24 years in California, I couldn't think of anywhere else to live. California was my home; all five of my children were born in California.

I could not, under any circumstances, take them to live in a country unknown to them. In June 2000, my husband and I separated. A month before, I had found him in Tijuana with another woman. In the 20 years that our marriage lasted. He had cheated on me many times. I had always forgiven him, but this time I couldn't do it. I returned to California with the youngest of my children. I never heard from my husband again. I knew that finally, a time of violence and abuse on his part had ended.

This was a time of betrayals and disappointments, on his part. He had committed a crime in California. We always visited him in prison because I wanted to keep the family together. Everything ended because of him. I am not to blame for anything. I had always asked for a miracle. I wanted my husband to be good to me and not get in trouble with the police anymore. I loved him for 20 years; we had five wonderful children that he never knew how to appreciate.

# Instrumental Music

Listening to instrumental music, such as that of Beethoven and Mozart, brings back memories of the cartoons I watched as a child in Mexico. In the cartoon programs the cat was always chasing the mouse. All this drama was done while we listened to classical music. Back then, my family was very poor and we couldn't afford music lessons, yet music was a constant presence in our home, thanks to cartoon programs and the radio.

I never knew traditional lullabies; instead, I fell asleep to songs like "Donde estas Corazon- Where are you Sweet heart" and "El Caballo Blanco- The White Horse" As an adult, I can say that I don't just like instrumental music—I am captivated by it. I still like Mariachi's music and romantic ballads, without forgetting the music that I found while watching some wonderful movies such as: Never on Sunday and The Sound of Music! When I hear those two melodies, I must sing, them while I'm driving.

One time, I was going to dinner with a boyfriend and start singing them. He immediately said: It's not karaoke time. I thought about dropping him and go alone to dinner! He immediately started laughing saying; it was a joke! My daughter Rose took music classes from elementary school and sang Whitney Houston's beautiful songs in high school.

She joined the university's school music program in 2002, and at the age of 20, she traveled to Italy with her university choir. I share this story to offer hope to those children who, like me, grew up without instrumental music. It's never too late to discover the joy that instrumental music can bring, regardless of one's age.

# Just a Cars' Story

Seven years ago, Henry and I found ourselves stranded in Acton, California. A friend had given us a lift but had to leave abruptly to pick up her children from school. I reached out to Sierra Toyota of Lancaster, and they dispatched a salesman to retrieve us. As we awaited his arrival, Henry became increasingly agitated, fretting over our inability to secure a vehicle. Our trusty 1986 minivan was on its last legs. I reassured him that Sierra Toyota appeared to be a reputable dealership, and if things didn't pan out, we'd simply visit another.

Nevertheless, Henry was distressed over the prospect of waiting for an hour. To ease his mind, I spun tales of the future, promising that in a decade, we'd simply call upon one of his siblings for a ride, perhaps even in a chauffeured limousine. "Really, mother?" he questioned, skepticism lacing his tone. I harbored grand aspirations for all my children, assuring him that these challenging times were temporary and that someday transportation woes would be a distant memory.

Ultimately, we didn't purchase a car from Sierra Toyota Lancaster, but they kindly returned us to Canyon Country. The following week, I acquired a 1999 Toyota Corolla from a different Toyota dealer. Henry, my youngest of five, began working at Valencia Target and attending College of the Canyons full-time at sixteen. Due to financial constraints, I allowed him to use my Corolla for a year. Two years prior, I managed to secure a car for him using my credit, and he has since been independently covering the car payments and insurance.

Owning his first car filled him with immense pride. Recently, Henry reached out for my assistance to co-sign for a new car. The dealership was ready to finalize the sale but required my endorsement as a co-signer. I obliged, and Henry proudly drove away in his BMW becoming the first in our family to own such a nice vehicle.

# Johnny

Have you ever watched the TV show M*A*S*H? One day, while I was watching the show, my young neighbor Johnny asked me, "Do you like the show, Maria?" "I like the show, Johnny," I replied. I find the show to be very funny and yet poignant at the same time. I had never thought that Johnny had seen the show before, and his response left me puzzled. "I like the show too," he said, "it reminds me of my country, Korea." After that, Johnny left the living room to play with my children.

I wondered if Johnny had watched the show with his parents. I never allowed my children to watch it because it contains many adult situations, and I don't think it's suitable for children. Johnny was born in Korea and came to this country as an infant. I suppose his parents must have watched the show and didn't have the heart to tell little Johnny that it's meant for adults. Or perhaps, Johnny watched the show while his parents were working. At that time, Johnny was eleven years old and a friend of my son. He embraced my family as his own, and we never minded. I have five children, and my friends' children were always welcome in my home.

One day, I opened my front door to find a bag full of groceries. Surprised, I called my husband to ask if he had left the groceries at the front door. He said he hadn't, and I spent the morning calling my friends to inquire about the bag of groceries. That evening, Johnny's mother called me to ask if Johnny was there. "He's here," I responded, "Do you want to talk to him?" "Just send him home, Maria," she said, "and I hope you enjoyed the groceries." I assured her that she didn't need to provide me with groceries.

"My son is always at your home; it's the least I can do," she replied. "I will always be grateful to your family for embracing my son as a friend." "Your son is such a delightful boy," I told her, "We are the fortunate ones to have him as a friend." Johnny faced troubles at the age of 15. Following his parents' divorce, his mother sought to set him straight. "He's going to live with his grandparents in Korea," she informed me. "Please," I implored, "don't send him yet.

Allow him to stay with my family for a week and reconsider your decision." The weary mother, working 16-hour days at her store, struggled to manage a rebellious teen. Johnny spent a week at my home, sharing a room with the boys, taking turns in the shower, and after a week, he pleaded with his mother to let him return. "I love this family," he declared, "but I want to live with you, Mom."

He vowed to behave, and the trip to Korea was called off. Johnny now serves in the Marines. He has embraced American citizenship and loves this country as his own. Johnny, will always have a special place in my heart. The young boy who frequently visited my home has grown into a man and is now far from us.

# Just not Right

My youngest daughter has returned home, having concluded a nearly three-year relationship. "I do care for him," she expressed, "but I cannot tend to him as though he were a child." His unwillingness to abandon his detrimental habits led to her departure. I welcome her back unquestioningly; she requires time alone. The pain of ending a relationship is familiar to me; her father left us six years ago.

Today's newspaper prompted me to write. It featured an article about a mother who passed away, leaving her eldest daughter responsible for five younger siblings. The daughter, once a student, forfeited her education to care for her ailing mother and siblings. Following her mother's death, a judge granted her custody of her siblings. Her photograph in the paper, surrounded by her siblings and smiling at the camera, belies the challenges ahead.

Love for her siblings is evident, but love alone may not suffice to keep a family united. I yearn to assure Lisa, the young guardian, she is deserving of more than the role of caregiver thrust upon her. It's truly appalling to burden such a young girl with five children. She needs the freedom to live her life, to pursue college and an education.

I've been in her shoes, caring for my mother's children and then my own five. Now at fifty, I'm still pursuing an education.

This girl is shouldering an immense burden. It's unjust to demand so much from her. I somehow long for a magical mirror to glimpse into Lisa' family twenty years hence. Her siblings are grown with families and careers of their own.

Lisa aged and embittered, having never pursued marriage or education, hears a sibling say, "You must do it, Lisa. Mother instructed you to care for us; don't expect our care now—it was your duty. "My youngest daughter refused to care for her boyfriend, ending a toxic relationship before it ensnared her.

But young Lisa can't utter 'no' to her siblings; breaking family bonds is often an arduous task. In Latino culture, it's customary for the eldest child to become the caregiver, a challenging concept for the culture to accept as unfair for a child, simply due to birth order. In royal families, the firstborn is heir to the throne, but in Latino families, the firstborn may be fated to lifelong care giving for younger siblings.

# Let the Stitches be Seen

When purchasing a beautiful dress, visible stitches are the last thing you want. The dress is costly, and the idea of friends noticing the stitches can be unsettling. They might simply see it as a dress, but to you, it's significant. The fear of ridicule for not inspecting the dress thoroughly looms. Indeed, some women desire to look stunning in a lovely dress, with all stitches neatly concealed beneath the fabric. Yet, there are other types of stitches, those that mark the skin.

These are the stitches we hide, for the cruelty of some husbands towards their wives forces them to live in constant terror. They fear the judgment of neighbors, the concern of parents, and the possibility of police intervention. Such events could lead to the husband's arrest, leaving the wife struggling to care for her children without employment or financial support. Day by day, she conceals her wounds, pleading with her husband to become a better partner and father.

# Los Angeles

Los Angeles is a stunning city that was once a part of Mexico—a long-forgotten piece of history for many. Today, this glamorous city is famed as the abode of movie stars, whose presence has skyrocketed LA's popularity. People are captivated by the lives of these stars, preferring their stories over confronting the harsh realities around us. Exhausted from juggling multiple jobs, we find solace in the escapism offered by the stars of the silver screen, guiding us like the celestial bodies above.

Take the movie "Bad Teacher," for instance; I, too, have watched it, initially seeking something valuable to share with my students. It took three months, but the humor eventually won me over, making me laugh so hard that I forgot my original intent. This is the essence of cinema—it's not about life lessons or doomsday prophecies; it's about thos 100 minutes of pure escape that are more cost-effective than therapy.

In the whirlwind of Los Angeles, one might argue that frequent movie-going is as essential as therapy. Los Angeles, the land of celebrities, is also home to the warm and welcoming Latino community, descendants of the city's original settlers, adding to the city's allure.

# Master

I observed her gazing at her husband in a manner reminiscent of how I once looked at mine. In silence, I expressed gratitude for no longer having a husband. My friend watched her husband, seeking to decipher his desires. She worships him, attending to him as a servant would to a master. It doesn't bother her; this lifestyle is familiar. I lived similarly for twenty years until I embraced freedom seven years ago. Now, I relish the liberty to sleep whenever I choose and dress as I wish. Above all, I cherish the freedom to pursue an education.

I ponder how many women still live as my friend does, their existence tethered to their spouses. They deeply love their husbands, yet the affection is not reciprocated equally. Adoration ought to be shared. I've raised my three sons to extend the same love and respect to women that all humans merit.

My sons understand that household duties are a shared responsibility and do not anticipate being served as masters. I aspire for my friend to impart this wisdom to her sons, fostering a generation that abandons the expectation of masterly treatment. With hope, the forthcoming generation will be the one to afford women the respect they rightfully deserve. Husbands and wives should be partners; never should a husband expect his wife to regard him as a master.

# My Son

Sometimes I wonder if I'm doing the same thing to my son that my mother did to me twenty years ago. She encouraged me to move to this country, perhaps with good intentions, believing I would find better opportunities here. I dreamed of becoming a lawyer. Unlike me, my mother didn't encourage Luisa or any of my other siblings. They graduated back home. It's been 15 years since I've seen them, and I often wonder if I ever will again.

Twenty years ago, I started my own family. My twins were born on 7-28-82 in Los Angeles. I have a son and a daughter. My daughter is studying at Loyola Marymount University, and my son is in the U.S. Army. Two months ago, I accompanied him to the recruitment office for information. They spoke of the army's benefits and opportunities. He took a test on 9-10-01, and a physical exam was scheduled for 9-15-01. Then, the tragic events of 9-11-01 unfolded. America was under attack, and suddenly, we were at war. I asked my son about his plans, whether he would still enlist. He confirmed he would.

Two weeks ago, I confided in my son about my illness and my reluctance to work the next day. He comforted me, promising to support me with his first paycheck. Understand me, I enjoy my job as a preschool teacher, but I am ill and need assistance. Now, I find myself in my mother's shoes, sending my child away, hoping for a better future. My mother never expressed pride in me, but I refuse to repeat that silence. I am immensely proud of my son; he is devoted to this country and will serve it with honor and courage.

# My Dream

I chose pen and paper over pots and pans, rejecting the old traditions of passive obedience. I pursued education against my mother's wishes, who envisioned for me a life mirroring hers—a perfect mother and wife. Instead, I embraced school, where my teachers inspired me with visions of becoming an educator like them. They instilled in me the belief that I could conquer the world, for my place was not confined to the four walls of a home.

At home, I waged a battle for being different. I yearned to master the written word, to craft my own narratives. My parents relented, allowing me to move to another county. There, I discovered the long-sought freedom. No longer was I suppressed; I was liberated to read and write. Though my hands weary from writing, my heart continually rejoices in a song of my realized dream.

# Missing California

I want to share this information about Melanie Safka. She is a singer, and had a hit in the Netherlands with "Beautiful People". She also performed at the Woodstock Festival in 1969 and the inspiration for her signature song, "Lay Down (Candles in the Rain)", apparently was inspired by the Woodstock audience lighting candles during her performance.

Melanie, also performs a lesser-known song titled "Carolina In My Mind," which includes lyrics like: "In my mind, I'm going to Carolina. Can't you see the sunshine? can't you just feel the moonshine? Ain't it just like a friend of mine to hit me from behind? Yes, I'm going to Carolina in my mind."

I discovered the CD at my son's place and brought it to my car to enjoy while driving to my doctor's appointments. Whenever I hear this song, I replace 'Carolina' with 'California' in my mind. This song resonates with immigrants who have left their families in pursuit of a better life, and with soldiers who are deployed far from home, yearning to return. Having moved to Washington State in December 2014 after 36 years in California, this song evokes not only the beauty of the state but also the cherished memories of my five children growing up there.

Relocating is a natural part of life, yet longing for a place you've grown to love, which now exists only in your memory, is deeply painful. I hope to grow fond of Washington just as my son has. He relocated there fourteen years ago, and although he misses California, he wouldn't exchange it for Washington. Washington State has become his home. At times, we have the liberty to choose our home; at other times, economic circumstances compel us to move to a different state or country. Despite the bittersweet emotions it evokes, I'll continue to listen to this song, unable to stop missing California.

# Mom's Potato Soup

I was reading "My Ántonia" by Willa Cather and found an interesting passage. In it, an elderly woman is harvesting potatoes from her garden for the family's dinner, assisted by her grandson. Together, they fill a small basket and head into their modest home to begin cooking. Recently, I enjoyed a lovely dinner with my eldest daughter, who treats me to a meal monthly. She shared her plans to start a new diet the next day. Although she doesn't seem overweight to me, she aspires to drop from a size eight to a size six.

We began our three-course meal with some tortilla soup. As our soup was served, I shared with my daughter that thirty years ago, during my time in Mexico, we often had only potato soup for dinner. She expressed surprise and curiosity about my life in Mexico. I recounted to her the recipe for my mother's savory potato soup: dicing eight large potatoes, browning them in a touch of olive oil, then simmering them with tomatoes, onions, garlic, and a sprinkle of flour for ten minutes until the soup was perfect for serving. In the past, grandmothers and mothers could nourish their children with nothing more than potatoes.

Today, we battle with weight issues as our meals often include two or three courses, followed by dessert. Resisting a plate laden with tamales, tacos, or enchiladas is a challenge. It's difficult to limit ourselves to just two tacos or enchiladas; we feel compelled to clear our plates. These are remarkable times; we no longer need to harvest potatoes from our garden to make potato soup for dinner. Instead, we simply order pizza or Chinese food with a phone call, yet this convenience comes at a steep cost.

One downside is our expanding waistlines, clogged arteries, and declining health. My daughter has requested my potato soup recipe, which I plan to email to her. She intends to make it someday, but for now, I'm happy that she invites me out for dinner. Together, we converse, dine, and reminisce about the days when women cooked daily to feed their lovely, hungry children.

# Message from your Mother

Dear children, I want to express my deepest love for you. I often ponder what my life would have been like without so many children, as there are many of you and only one of me. We've experienced tough times, but also moments of joy. Growing up with you was special to me, as I never had a childhood myself. My mother needed me for chores, so I couldn't be a child. Your own friends became my family, filling a void in my life. Assisting you with homework was a joy, as I always yearned for education.

Recall, Richie, when I completed your history paper? Your teacher praised you, unaware it was my doing. You all kept me occupied and gave my life purpose. Making friends was hard, as I never found someone who shared my passion for learning. I still face this challenge. Please forgive my impatience and outbursts; I struggled to contain them. My love for you is boundless, and I regret not saying it enough.

# Never Give Up

I strongly believe that an education will help us to achieve our dreams. This writing is about the importance of education and the tenacity to never give up on your dreams. It emphasizes that women, now more than ever, need access to education. Despite numerous interruptions in my studies at College of the Canyons, I persistently returned to my classes. The thought of a life without a degree, confined to cleaning houses, was unimaginable to me. I held onto the belief that, although my dream often seemed unattainable, it was achievable.

I am eager to share this message with those who value the well-being of others, particularly with women. It's not sufficient to merely desire an education for our children; we can achieve it together. I urge you to share my essay with anyone who values education. In this world, we are united; changing one life at a time represents an investment in our collective future. Everyone deserves the opportunity for a brighter future. I am convinced that education is the key to one day, realizing our dreams.

# Older Children and their Parents

When children depart, where do they venture? Are they off to purchase pastries? But no, thrice no, for older children have outgrown grandma's pastries and hot chocolate, now they are favoring margaritas instead! They vow to return as they leave, weary of the grown-ups' world. They chase joy, yet leave trails of sorrow for their parents. The parents weep at the sight of the empty nest, the fledglings gone without farewells—a heartrending tragedy.

Some parents yearn for lifelong bonds, while children crave liberty to lead their own lives. "They will come back," the elders say, versed in life's tales. They, too, once wept, but their tears dried, and joy eventually found its way. We must await the brighter days, await them with love. For nothing is novel beneath the sun. The tussle between offspring and progenitors persists, yet time remains unforgiving. The youth revel in their vernal bloom, but winter spares none, meting out retribution and settling bygone scores.

# One Cold Night

The date was 12-22-05; the time, 9:30 PM; the place, College of the Canyons. I was walking to my car. Many times, I've parked in the morning and forgotten where by evening. Tired and cold, I didn't want the struggle of searching for my car. Reaching the parking lot and seeing my car, I almost cried. It was the lone car in the vast lot. The only one! I thought to myself, "Was I the last student to leave C.O.C. that night?"

I pondered the approaching Christmas, set to be another somber one. No funds for gifts, celebrations, or parties. We would stay in, dine together, as we had for the past five years. The next day, a check from my school arrived. With this money, I bought presents for my family and self-published a small book titled "My Graduation," where I advocate for education and encourage reading and writing.

The journey isn't easy. I'm still attending school, still facing challenges, but my days seem lighter. My stories of pursuing education later in life aim to inspire hope in others. The mirror reflects my age; my spirit feels youthful. I yearn to be 25 again, to accomplish what I once couldn't. My dream is to reach those like me, striving daily for a better life for themselves and their families.

# One More Story

In this piece, I express my desire for my children's education as well as my own.

Assisting them with their homework made me appreciate the remarkable work teachers do in schools and the need for bilingual educators, not just for language proficiency but to understand the living conditions of some Latino children. In my writing, I aim to inspire a desire to assist others through learning a new language. Having bilingual assistants is beneficial, especially if they perform well, as I have experienced firsthand. Yet, the classroom's lead—the teacher—misses out on much by not communicating with the children. Why is there a reluctance to learn new languages in America?

Europeans often speak two or three languages due to their proximity to other nations. America is near Canada and Mexico, yet there's little interest in learning French or Spanish. There's a strong defense of the English language here. I respect English too; it was the medium of my entire education. When I moved to California at 23, I began translating 40 to 50 words daily, worked, and attended English classes. I understand the challenge, dear Latin brothers, but it's not insurmountable. My advice, as an educator, is to become bilingual and thus help more people.

# Once

Once, a long time ago, we shared the same womb. I emerged as the eldest, and you, the youngest. Your memories of growing up are filled with joy, while mine are so dark they compel me to voice them. I've been silent for years, living in fear, but now I feel the need to share my harrowing past, knowing I'm not alone in having suffered abuse. I harbored the secret alone yearning to erase the memories of beatings and the names she called me.

I was just a child! She was my mother, expected to love and protect me. I questioned God, "Why me?" but no answer came. The physical abuse ceased when I turned fourteen, perhaps because she recognized in me a burgeoning strength. She never laid hands on me again, yet the verbal assaults persisted. Please, don't ask me to pose for a family photo. Don't question my lack of affection for our mother as you do.

Oh, how I wish to trade places, to be the younger sibling just once, to experience the mother you cherish. Once, dear sister, we slumbered side by side within the womb, but now our lives diverge sharply. You are touched by love. I am scarred by hate, and my memories grant me no peace, not even for a moment.

# Picking up Seashells

The interminable hours, pass and I am here in the living room waiting for my love, Maria, to wake up. My love drove for three hours coming down from our trip to Carpinteria, California. It was my first time visiting this place, but not for her. She was not tired from the trip, she was emotionally tired because Maria was overwhelmed by the memories that this trip brought to her aching heart

While she sleeps, I remember our walk by the seashore. While walking, Maria picked some seashells that were scattered on the beach. She didn't keep them. She gave them to a group of children that were making sand castles on the beach. Maria's children are grown and they live so far away from her. They used to visit her very often, but lately they stopped coming to see her. Carpinteria beach was the place where her children used to play and swim during their summer vacation.

I went to the room and woke her up. We had a nice breakfast together; I want to help her to make new memories with me by her side. Her happiness was to take care of her children. I will take care of her from now on, to give her all the happiness that she deserves. My own children are grown; we are two lonely souls, who deserved a chance to be happy one more time.

# Reading is Important

Being born into a culture that undervalues reading can make it challenging to embrace the habit, as it often means standing alone against one's own culture. Although Mexican culture is imbued with traditions that value hard work, it unfortunately views reading as a frivolous activity. A core tradition is the respect for one's parents, placing children who are passionate about reading in a dilemma: honor their parents by abandoning their books or continue reading against their wishes.

Tragically, when a parent passes away or leaves the family, the responsibility to provide falls on the older children, robbing them of their childhood and the financial ability to purchase books. The cultural bias in Mexico, regrettably, leans towards men, expecting women to remain at home to manage domestic duties and care for children. Consequently, older daughters often have so many household responsibilities that finding time for reading is neither feasible nor permitted.

Women are often viewed as future mothers and wives, expected to learn cooking and housekeeping. Those who read books are labeled as rebels. Personally, reading distinguished me from my family. My mother deemed it a waste of time and burdened me with chores. I would secretly read after completing them, hiding my books to prevent her from discarding them. What she considered trash was my treasure.

I aspire to transform this culture and inspire women who cherish reading. Reading is not just a part of my life; it is my life. Having self-published five books, I now share my stories. My goal is to cultivate a reading culture and improve Mexican culture. While traditions are valuable, those that deprive eager readers of books should be challenged to uphold the freedom to read.

# Red Hair

I wasn't born with red hair; my natural color was black. However, upon discovering numerous gray strands, I chose to eliminate the gray. Everyone seemed to admire my red hair, or perhaps they were just being kind by saying it suited me. I maintained the red hue for a decade, but last month, I felt the need for a change and reverted to black. At sixty years old, if I stop dyeing, my hair would be entirely gray. It's a natural part of aging to lose our hair pigment.

While some embrace their graying hair and never conceal it, I cannot stand mine, so I continue to color it every six weeks. I just finished watching the movie "Jenny's Wedding" where two women wish to marry each other. Marriage is a significant step; it's natural to want your family and loved ones present. In the film, Jenny's parents initially disapprove of her decision, leading to arguments and hurt feelings. However, by the movie's end, the family resolves their differences and joyfully celebrates the union of the two women.

I long for life to be as simple as changing one's hair color or as it is portrayed in films, where people endure hardship simply because they desire what many take for granted: a family. I have been married twice, and although my parents could not attend either ceremony due to living abroad, I still felt their love from afar. Family life can bring joy or challenges; yet having a family or belonging to one is a fundamental right that should be protected and encouraged for all.

# Remembering my Parents

My parents are in their nineties and I haven't seen them in 15 years. I went to Mexico in 2010 and in 2016, but I couldn't see them then. They were visiting some other members of my family living in another state at the same time of my visit. When I go to Mexico, I only stay for a few days, because I have to go back to work. I don't speak to them very often because talking to them makes me very sad. They are always asking me to come to see them or them want to come and visit me.

We gazed at the horizon, hoping to see you arrive, but you didn't come that day. You had stayed on to work another shift. At that time, there was no phone for you to inform us that you were working overtime. As we matured into teenagers, Mom managed to ease her anxiety slightly about your absence. We reassured her repeatedly that you were fine and would return home from work the next day.

She would then become silent and fall asleep. Occasionally, it felt as though she was the child and we were responsible for her care, especially when she secluded herself in her room, not to emerge until the following day. Dad's absence in the home greatly impacted us, even if it went unspoken. Although ten children were raised by two parents, there were times it felt as if we had grown up on our own. We had parents, but we looked after one another, with dad always at work and mom perpetually engaged in household chores and confined to her room.

# Sebastian and David

My name is Maria Morales, and I have been a teacher for the past 10 years. Throughout my career, I have assisted numerous students, but two in particular were very dear to me. They are Sebastian and David (pseudonyms). Both were sociable, yet I consistently reminded them to converse outside rather than inside the classroom. At twelve years old, both boys shared a passion for soccer, giving them much to discuss.

It was essential for their focus to remain on education, so I separated them to prevent classroom chatter. One sat at the front near my desk, and the other at the back. The boys pleaded to stay together, but I understood the necessity of distance for their benefit. I assured them they could collaborate during class work time. Eager to work together, they frequently inquired if it was time for class work.

I am delighted to report that both attended college together, one pursuing medicine and the other teaching. While students enjoy socializing, they must recognize the importance of class time. It is during these moments that they receive an education, equipping them with the necessary tools to fulfill their aspirations and become professionals, just like Sebastian and David.

# Survivor

The writer, Jim Marquez, wrote an essay called "The Girl in the Café a Portrait". His essay describes perfectly how much suffering a woman endures when she is married to man who sees her as his property. I know about suffering, I know about violence, I was a victim of domestic violence. In his essay, this young woman is afraid to talk to people, or look at other men. She is waiting for her husband in a café. She was not there to enjoy a cup of coffee or a relaxing conversation. Her purpose in being was to meet her master; her owner.

I know how hard it is for people to think that in these times we can find slaves. But I really think that a woman who marries a man and is afraid to leave him or fears for her life is a true slave. As a survivor of domestic violence, I can testify in favor of these women. I was one of them. I waited for almost twenty years for a miracle to happen. I hoped that my husband would change and one day sees me as his loving wife and partner and not his property.

I am a lucky survivor, but there are a lot of women in this horrible situation. I hope that if you see yourself in this essay, you will do something about it. Domestic violence shouldn't be treated as something that happens to losers, or to women that don't have self esteem. Domestic violence happens more often than we think; I know it because I am a domestic violence survivor.

# Sisters

You might think, "Here's yet another story about sisters and their bond." However, this short story delves into the sacrifices we made as sisters to ensure our family's survival. My name is Maria, and I am the eldest of seven sisters. As the eldest, it fell upon me to watch over the rest of them. At times, this responsibility was daunting, as I was but a child myself, tasked with caring for my mother's children. My mother wished to keep me at home to continue this role, but our neighbors insisted that I must attend school, as it was the law.

Fearful of potential consequences, she enrolled me in school at the age of seven. This marked a significant turning point in my life. School introduced me to a new world. My teachers were kind and compassionate, treating me with respect and dignity. I felt empowered to speak out and participate, answering questions from my textbooks. They motivated me to pursue my studies and to learn. For the first time, I encountered people who viewed me as an individual, not merely as someone to command.

When my first sister was born, I was three years old. At six, she relied on me, then nine, to escort her to school. Luisa, a timid and frequently ill child, resisted school during winter. I would inform her teacher of her illness, receiving assignments for her to complete at home, which I supervised. Remarkably, she passed her class despite missing over two months of school.

I also significantly aided my sister Catalina. I registered her for school at five, confident in her readiness, as she had learned to read by listening to our other sisters. I took it upon myself to engage my sisters in reading and singing post-school, fostering their education. My mother's family grew, and by the time I was seventeen and Patricia was born, I felt overwhelmed and resentful. Desiring college, I felt confined in a home swarming with children—her children.

I harbored no resentment towards my sisters, but towards her, for insisting it was my duty to assist the family. As the eldest, the responsibility fell on me. At eighteen, I secured factory work, sewing by day and aiding my sisters' studies by night. Despite the burden, I found joy in it, unknowingly training for my current role as a teacher. My sisters were my first students. They trusted me with their education, and I never failed them.

I encouraged them to make the impossible possible because from a home with no books we managed to learn and pass our classes. I went to their graduation ceremonies to witness the miracle of perseverance and dedication. Seven girls that were born in a family where the two parents never went to school are helping so many people thanks to their education. Two of my sisters are doctors, two are secretaries; one of them is a teacher, just like me! Each of us carries a flame within our souls and hearts, ignited by our teachers. We are all capable of supporting our families during these tough economic times.

Unlike my mother, we do not stay at home; we have much to accomplish. We work and we also volunteer in our communities. We are constantly advocating for education, for all. My story is one of family and love, and a passion for pursuing education despite the odds. My sisters are warriors and survivors, embodying the belief that good things come to those who are good. We have endured many challenges together, yet we always believed better times lay ahead. I am filled with pride for my sisters; they are in Mexico, and I am in California. Though we live in separate countries, our shared childhood memories forever unite us.

# Sweet Caroline

I met her a long time ago. My son, Trinidad, came home from school one day and said, "Mom, you have to meet Devin's grandma; she dresses just like you." Indeed, I met her, and our friendship blossomed because Caroline was always willing to listen, and I valued her advice. She cared for Devin, her grandson, while his mother was at work. She would be outside Devin's school an hour before it ended.

When I asked why she arrived so early, she explained that she wanted to avoid traffic and arriving early allowed her to catch up on her reading. We share a passion for reading. Sometimes, after I finish my books from the public library, she borrows them and then returns them. Once, she inquired about how I find my books, and I told her that I don't find the books; rather, the books find me.

She spent her career as a secretary and continued to work by caring for her grandson every day after retirement. "I love my grandson," she would say, "he's the reason I wake up in the morning." Her husband passed away when she was sixty-five, and she never remarried. I once asked her how she manages to live alone, as the thought frightens me. She replied that living alone doesn't bother her because her family always calls and her friends frequently visit.

I visited my dear sweet Caroline yesterday to thank her for 13 years of friendship and to let her know how much it means to me. Caroline is starting a new chapter in her life; she's moving to a nursing home. She left her home of 45 years last week. It's difficult to let go of your entire life when you're no longer strong enough to do things on your own. I invited Caroline to dinner, but she declined. She's not ready to go out yet; she's grieving the loss of her independence, the plants she cherished, and her neighbors. She needs time to adjust to her new life. I only pray that my sweet Caroline finds the strength to continue living.

# Stray Cats

Did you know that attempting to pet a stray cat may result in it hissing at you? Stray cats are not accustomed to the gentle touch of a human hand and may attack out of instinct. As a teaching assistant, I overheard some children using profanity in Spanish last week. I questioned them, "How can such foul language come from your mouths in a classroom that deserves respect?" They retorted that they spoke that way at home. I explained that such language, even if used at home, was not permissible at school.

They insisted on their right to be in the classroom with their teacher's permission. They threatened to inform the teacher that I wanted them out of the classroom. I apologized for my advice, pleading, "Please don't tell the teacher; I don't want to lose my job." I left them be and returned to my desk. Upon the teacher's return, I reported the incident. She assured me that she does not allow foul language in her classroom, regardless of the language.

I implored her to overlook the incident to avoid any trouble. It is disheartening when someone like, myself feels intimidated by a group of stray cats. Indeed, stray cats are unaware of a human's gentle touch. Regrettably, some students may never discern the difference between a world filled with kindness and one inhabited by stray cats.

# Sharing

My elderly neighbor was outside his apartment. I sighed at the thought of engaging in conversation; I merely wanted to greet him and continue on. However, he craves interaction so much that a simple "Hi" is never sufficient. Upon exchanging greetings, he inquired about my destination. "I'm off to the library and the store," I replied. "You don't need the library; I have a vast collection of movies and books you can borrow anytime," he offered. I politely declined his offer, explaining my need to find Spanish books for my class at the library.

My neighbor, 83 and without family, is always eager for a chat with the neighbors. "Why not donate some of your movies or books to the library?" I suggested. "You must be joking," he retorted, "my books are my life, and my movies are too valuable to give away. "It was just an idea," I responded. "The library is always open to donations." After bidding him farewell, I departed.

Reflecting on my neighbor, his living room brimming with books and films, yet no one to share them with, contrasted with the library that shares its wealth with all. The public library feels like a second home to me; I only purchase books when the library doesn't carry them. For class-required readings, I first seek them at the library, which can even source them from other county libraries if necessary.

The next day, my neighbor surprised me with a visit, offering a bag full of books for donation to the library. He had decided to open his heart and share his treasures. It often seems that sharing our knowledge, possessions, and time is one of our purposes on this planet. Indeed, sharing is challenging. We hold onto our belongings as tightly as a toddler clutches their toys.

# Substitute Teachers

Much like a homeless person who carries their possessions at all times, substitute teachers tote their books and pencils from one school to another. We are educators without a classroom to call our own, dreaming of the day we will be appointed to a permanent position. We envision a future where we have our own students to mentor, guiding them towards their aspirations. Until then, we commit ourselves to the role of being present in the classroom, known as substitute teachers.

At times, we fill in for a single day; other times, for an entire week. We may repeatedly substitute for the same teacher at the same school. Occasionally, a teacher may fall ill for weeks or months, or they may need to care for a family member over an extended period. In these instances, substitute teachers step in to ensure that education continues uninterrupted. These are challenging times for substitute teachers, as we often encounter students who misbehave upon learning their regular teacher is absent. It's important to note that most schools are very supportive of substitutes, even referring to us as guest teachers.

The administrative staff usually greets us warmly and supports our role in the classroom. However, there are instances where some schools take the side of disruptive students and hold substitutes accountable for any issues that arise. Many of my friends suggest I quit substitute teaching and seek a different career, arguing that it's not a stable job. Having been a substitute for six years, I find joy in my work, yet I ponder whether to heed their counsel. Recently, I inquired of another substitute teacher how long they had been in the profession.

They replied, "Ten years," a duration I find hard to envision for myself. In two months, I'll be relocating from California to Washington State, hoping for better fortune. My friend Sofia, a substitute teacher for seven years, advised me to stay, citing the students' need for us. I recognize their need, yet now is the moment to prioritize my own. The delightful students who heeded my guidance and brought me immense joy throughout my tenure as a substitute teacher will be dearly missed.

# The Public Library

In times past, every beach boasted a lighthouse, serving as a beacon to guide sailors. Amidst storms that veiled the skies, when sailors lost their way in the ocean's expanse, the lighthouse was their beacon of hope. Similarly, Plazas were once the gathering grounds for philosophers who engaged with the public, sharing their wisdom on life's philosophies – among them, the renowned Socrates, Aristotle, and Plato.

However, the era of lighthouses has waned, replaced by modern technology that aids sailors. The Plazas, too, have faded, no longer hosting gatherings of philosophers. Today, the public library has become the new beacon and gathering place. It is here that people come together to learn about figures like Socrates and Aristotle. The public library enriches community life with its myriad services and the assistance of its dedicated staff. Among these services is internet access, a vital resource during challenging economic times. The library also lends movies, allowing patrons to take them home for a week with the option to renew. Music CDs are available for borrowing, and a vast selection of books awaits children, teens, and adults alike.

Furthermore, the public library invites speakers to share their knowledge, continuing the tradition of enlightenment. While lighthouses and Plazas belong to history, the public library remains a pivotal part of our present and future. By frequenting the library, we keep it vibrant and uphold the cherished tradition of library visits. For many, a trip to the public library is akin to visiting a dear friend, and the anticipation of returning is always present.

# Ten Minutes

When my five children were young, they used to help me by reading aloud. I was often busy in the kitchen cooking for them and enjoyed listening to stories. I asked them to read to me for just ten minutes a day, which also counted towards their reading assignments for homework. Among my five children, I recall one who always resisted when it was his turn to read. He would complain, saying he hated reading because it took too long to finish a book and he preferred watching TV, especially "Gilligan's Island." I insisted that he needed to practice his reading as it was the only way to improve.

He was so reluctant that he repeatedly asked, "How many more minutes, Mom?" Now, that son is no longer ten years old; he's twenty-seven and has developed a love for reading. Recently, he spoke to me about a book series he was reading. He discovered the first book at the public library, borrowed the second from a friend, and requested the third from the library. The series is called "The Girl with the Tattoo."

As mothers, we strive to instill values and morals in our children. We can't predict their futures, but we hope they'll remember the lessons learned with us. I'm overjoyed that after all those years of reading together, my grown children now recognize the importance of reading. They read for pleasure, without any prompting. Some even call me to discuss books like Harry Potter or other new reads.

# The Picture

An old photograph rests permanently on his dresser, its faces barely discernible now. Captured over sixty years ago, it features his mother and her relatives—a small assembly of individuals who once formed a family. His recollections of his mother are filled with warmth. After his father's passing when he was merely three, she single-handedly raised three children, with him being the youngest. From a tender age, he witnessed her toil; she laundered and ironed for affluent families. His education was brief, as the fields demanded his labor. Eager to work, he yearned to relieve his mother so she could rest.

Despite his prayers for her well-being, arthritis ravaged her hands, and she succumbed to the strain of hard work at a young age. His adoration for his mother endures, even in her absence. "I'm certain she's in heaven," he confided in me, "watching over me from above." The aged picture will occupy its place on his dresser eternally, yet he requires no photograph to envision his mother. She resides forever in his heart, sculpted by the same loving hands that welcomed him into the world.

# The Coupons

Mrs. Brown was a delightful elderly lady who taught me the art of saving money with coupons. Thirty years ago, as her caregiver, one of my tasks was to accompany her on grocery shopping trips; it was there I learned the value of couponing. Now, on a Saturday night, I find myself clipping coupons. I purchase the Sunday edition of the Los Angeles Times on Saturdays, so I'm prepared for the next day's shopping. Thanks to couponing, my children always had an abundance of cereal and cookies.

I recall when my children were younger, they would return from school with envelopes brimming with coupons. On Mother's Day, some thoughtful teachers would have students create coupons for their mothers, symbolizing their love and gratitude. Each coupon, a simple piece of paper, might say, "Good for vacuuming the house" or "Good for washing the family car." The joy on my children's faces as I read each coupon aloud was priceless. They kept their promises, fulfilling every single one. They were such wonderful little helpers.

Just last month, my daughters treated me to dinner and a movie. We shared a delightful evening at Mimi's Café and watched the film titled "Mamma Mia." Our family has always cherished the music of Abba, ever since I discovered a cassette at the Valencia library twenty-five years ago, which turned us all into fans. My children, now adults, don't take me out as often as I'd like. They're preoccupied with their own families, leaving their mother feeling a bit lonely, eagerly anticipating the holidays to reunite.

Sometimes, I wish I could create coupons for my adult children, offering them for their birthdays. One might read, "Good for dinner with Mother," another, "Good for breakfast with Mother," valid throughout the year without an expiration date. In tiny letters beneath, they would find a piece of advice: "Don't let 'Father Time' rob you of moments with your mother before you have the chance to use these."

# The Old Bookcase

Inside the classroom stood an old bookcase, a small green one with just six shelves. It was so diminutive it could only accommodate seven to ten books on each shelf. The bookcase was barren, as if awaiting the arrival of books. This old bookcase stirred memories of a similar one we had in Mexico fifty years ago, identical in its dark green hue and size.

In Mexico, that bookcase never held books; instead, my mother used it to store her dishes. She was quite particular about these dishes, guarding them zealously and forbidding us from touching them. These dishes were reserved for family dinners, which occurred once or twice a year due to the great distance her family lived from us. On those occasions, she would cook tamales and serve them on her cherished dishes.

The dishes weren't fancy or costly. They were an assortment of pieces collected over time, mismatched gifts from her family. Sometimes it was a cup, other times a bowl or a salad plate, each bought from the market for a peso or two. To my mother, however, they symbolized her family's affection. I despised these dishes for they represented something beyond my comprehension.

One day, while cleaning these dishes, I accidentally broke one. Blood from my hand began to fill the sink. Not waiting for assistance, I grabbed a kitchen towel and fled from the house, terrified of my mother's reaction. I didn't stay to explain that it was an accident, that I hadn't broken her dish intentionally. After three hours, I returned home. The towel had staunched the bleeding, but my hand was still in pain.

I hoped her anger had subsided, that she wouldn't punish me. But my hopes were in vain; she still lashed out. I sometimes wonder if her dishes held the same value to her as books do to me. I cherish my books, yet unlike her, I don't keep them as mere decorations. I share them with friends and students, and sometimes, I even give them away. Books are meant to be read and to travel to other homes and hands.

# The Little Chicks

Recently, while searching for new books for my Spanish students, I stumbled upon a quaint book titled "Los Pollitos" (The Little Chicks). I pulled it from the shelf and began to read, only to discover that it was about a lullaby I had often sung to my children to help them sleep. For years, I've carried a sense of guilt for not reading bedtime stories to my children. I never read to them because there were always so many tasks to complete. Instead of reading, I sang to them. We would repeat the lullaby "Los Pollitos" until they drifted off to sleep.

Caring for my five children was a joy; we spent time together at the park, the library, and the local swimming pool. I was fortunate to have those years with them when I wasn't working. I had always hoped to be a stay-at-home parent, but financial obligations meant I had to return to work. Juggling child-rearing, work, and school left little time for reading. However, we sang together frequently. They inherited my love for music. If you can read to your children, please do so. But if you can't, sing to them. They'll feel the love and security in your care, just as the little chicks do under the mother hen's wing.

# The Best

One day, our cat Oscar was scavenging food from the trash can. My son Henry promptly removed him, admonishing, "You should know better than to eat from the trash." Henry is very attentive to Oscar's needs. Having been a part of our family for twelve years, Oscar receives his care and attention. Henry ensures he is well-fed and his space is clean.

At times, I ponder whether parents, in their exasperation with their grown children, might react as Henry did with Oscar. We nurture them to excel, shield them from myriad perils, and pause our own lives to ensure their welfare. Yet, some adults resort to 'eating from trash'—not literally from bins, but by indulging in drugs, engaging in violence, and harming themselves and others.

# Vanessa and her Beautiful Mother

While tutoring my student Vanessa in math, she began speaking Spanish. I gently reminded her to continue in English, explaining that I reserve my Spanish for students who aren't fluent in English, and she was. Vanessa shared that she also speaks English at home, encouraged by her mother, who will soon take her citizenship exam and wants her daughter's help with English. It was heartwarming to learn about a family learning English together. Often in Latino families, only the children learn English, leaving them to translate for their parents.

Vanessa's family is exceptional in their collective effort to learn English. This mutual support mirrors the assistance I provide to my students. Learning doesn't only happen in school; it continues at home. Mastering a new language is challenging but achievable. I advise practicing the second language frequently, and home is an ideal environment for this. Vanessa's mother is likely to succeed in her citizenship test, becoming a new citizen. It's logical for her to learn English, anticipating that she and her daughter, as future citizens, will converse in English.

# Victor

Victor was one of my students. At that time, I wasn't a teacher, but a teacher's assistant. Although my students addressed me as a teacher, I encouraged them to call me Mrs. Morales, as Mrs. Nichols was their actual teacher and I was her aide. Yet, they insisted that I was their teacher because I helped them learn. It was 1997, and I was working as a TA while attending College of the Canyons in the evenings. With spring break approaching, I inquired about my students' plans for the class-free week. They shared that they would be staying home since their parents were working.

I proposed a field trip to The Ronald Reagan Presidential Library in Simi Valley, which excited my six students so much they promised to seek their parents' permission. Later that evening, I called their parents to confirm permission and informed them that the trip was a reward for their children's excellent performance. The following Wednesday, I took my five children to Valencia Mall, then, went to pick up my students. Before heading to The Ronald Reagan Presidential Library, we stopped at McDonald's to pick up six Happy Meals and a salad for me. I ordered the food to go because I wanted my students to enjoy the Library's gardens while eating.

Three boys and three girls, eager to see the museum, quickly finished their meals. Inside the museum, my students examined each exhibit with wonder and surprise. Although my own children were tired of visiting the Presidential Library, my students were excited to discover the treasures it offered. Two hours flew by quickly, and we bid farewell to the library. On our way back home to Santa Clarita, I asked my students for a favor: to write a paragraph about the museum, specifically about the one thing that impressed them the most, due the following week when we returned to school.

The next week, only one student submitted the assignment. Victor had written about the Berlin Wall and the significance of freedom to him. He didn't just write a paragraph; he filled the entire page. At the bottom, he affixed the sticker provided as confirmation that his admission fee was paid. Reading

Victor's assignment moved me to tears. He had listened to me, even though I wasn't his teacher. My students inspired me to persevere in school and pursue teaching.

Their dedication and kindness have greatly enriched my life. I visited Victor recently; he's now 27 years old. I presented him with a copy of my book and my contact number, hoping to stay in touch. Victor aspires to attend college and become an architect. Now, it's my opportunity to mentor him and reassure him that in this wonderful country, education is attainable, and we should never cease to believe in our dreams.

# Walking Everywhere

Walking to school never bothered me, as all my peers did the same. Despite the distance, I was eager to see my teachers and hear their tales. My third-grade teacher, Margarita, had a face as angelic as those painted on church walls. I admired her silently, learning early to conceal my feelings, as expressing fondness for a teacher seemed inappropriate. The park was my frequent retreat from our cramped two-room home, a break from my mother's vigilant gaze and the endless chores.

I persuaded her to let me take my younger siblings to the park under the guise of giving her rest. This ruse granted me a slice of paradise, allowing me to play while supervising them. Reflecting on those days, it's astonishing how content we were despite our poverty. As a child, the sting of poverty is often overshadowed by the joy found in simple pleasures like school, a park, or a market. I sometimes ponder whether I'll ever see those familiar places again.

# We are Having a Party

While waiting in line to pay for groceries, I noticed two children in front of me counting their money. "We don't have enough," one said. "We need to put the candy back," the other agreed. Observing their small basket filled with a small pizza, a large bottle of soda, a bag of chips, and candy, I saw them remove the candy and continue counting. "Are these groceries for dinner?" I asked, feeling sad they couldn't afford their items. "No," they replied, "it's for a party, but we can't afford the candy, so we're putting it back." Relieved, I offered to pay for the candy if they allowed me to go ahead.

They happily agreed, and the candy returned to their basket, saving their party. As they joyfully made plans, I pondered if we could learn from their simple happiness over a few dollars and a celebration of friendship. After leaving the store, I headed to the post office to send my son in Iraq some American treats. He loved pizza, cookies, and candies as a child, and though I can't send pizza, the cookies and candies might remind him of home. He's told me his friends eagerly await these parcels. Just as the two boys in America cherish their friendship, our soldiers, far from home, are reminded that their families think of them and eagerly await the day we reunite.

# Working While She Went to School

During my time in the California onion fields, I would carry my portable radio. Not knowing English then, I immersed myself in Mexican music all day. It transported me to Mexico in my mind. While my body toiled, filling countless boxes with onions, my spirit roamed free. I conversed with my mother, siblings, and teachers. I strolled through the streets of Monterrey, buying fruits and tortillas for my family. The separation from them was unbearable; they were my world, yet poverty forced me to leave my homeland.

My youngest sister was just six when I departed. Her pleading eyes haunt me still, "Don't go, Maria. Stay here." But it was my duty to support them. My sacrifices ensured she never toiled under the harsh sun; she finished high school and then got married. She remains unaware of the grueling work I endured in California's fields from dawn till dusk. The music was my solace, as my soul was elsewhere, leaving only my weary body behind to labor in the sun.

# Wonderful Lady

Six years ago, I met Cindy when she was seeking a babysitter for her son Timothy. Her eldest son, Mathew, was only five and already active in show business. As a dedicated stay-at-home mom, Cindy needed someone to look after Timmy while she accompanied Mathew to his TV show and commercial tapings. At that time, I was a full-time student at College of the Canyons, searching for a part-time job. I came across Cindy's ad in the newspaper and decided to respond.

From the moment I entered her home, Cindy welcomed me warmly. Despite the stereotypes of movie stars being difficult, Cindy was incredibly grounded. She took pride in maintaining her home, although she had help with the heavy cleaning once a week. Cindy made it clear that my role was to care for her sons, not the household. She generously offered me anything from her fridge and asked me to list any special items I might need so she could purchase them for me. When I mentioned my preference for a bit of cream in my coffee, she surprised me the following week with two bottles of vanilla coffee creamer—one for her house and one for me to take home.

Cindy's kindness will forever be etched in my memory for the way she opened her home and trusted me with her precious boys, making me feel valued. Sharing my experiences as a sitter is something I cherish, especially since it allowed me to complete my homework while the children were occupied with television. I'm grateful for the loving families like Cindy's who supported me as I cared for their children. Thanks to them, my dream of becoming a teacher has been realized. Through this essay, I express my heartfelt gratitude to Cindy, for her exceptional kindness; she truly is one-of-a-kind.

# Women

Twenty-five years ago, two women left the hospital; I was one of them. The other was an elderly woman clutching a prescription. "Is something wrong?" I inquired. "My prescription," she replied, "It's $15.00." Lacking the funds, she departed empty-handed. Back then, I had money—not a lot, but enough to spare $15.00. Yet, I didn't offer it. Instead, I went grocery shopping for my family.

I had visited the hospital to consent to a surgery that would prevent further pregnancies. I was expecting my fifth child, who was to be my last. Today, I found myself at the pharmacy. I inquired about the cost of my prescription before filling it, as I lacked insurance. "I'll give you a discount," the pharmacist said gently. The cost was $15.00, but I hesitated, saying I'd consider it. She agreed to prepare it and keep it on hold for two weeks. Having paid $50.00 for the doctor's visit, I doubted the necessity of the prescription.

I decided if I felt worse in a day or two, I'd purchase it. I had bought a cream for my skin rash five days prior and planned to use it up before considering the prescription. Times are tough now. A quarter-century ago, I had a husband and a family; now, I'm alone, managing a stringent budget. I never used to budget, buying whatever I fancied, never imagining a day without money. I've become the old woman from my past, fearful of a bleak future, struggling to meet my basic needs.

# Who are the Best Children?

Most mothers would claim their own as the best. Yet, I once believed mine were anything but good. I come from a generation where obedience was demanded, and punishment followed disobedience. Today, my fifteen-year-old son, Ritchie, is painting the house, with his younger brother, Henry, assisting by fetching water for drinking or brush cleaning. Henry shadows Richie just as he once did following their father.

My husband has left us for another life in Mexico. Inside, Kelly and Rose manage the kitchen and bathrooms, while Trinidad, my eldest at seventeen, handles the vacuuming. Amidst laundry, I'm on calls with realtors; the house must sell since the mortgage is unaffordable without my husband. Previously, chores were a battleground of complaints and accusations of meanness for not allowing leisure until tasks were completed. I'd argue that our large family needed to support one another.

They yearned for television, video games, and lazy weekend mornings. Now, my five children unite in our efforts, enabling me to seek a smaller home for us. Our family of seven is no more; one has departed. Rose will soon attend Loyola Marymount University, and her twin enlisted in the army. They stand with me, striving to preserve our family bond. They may be maturing, but in my eyes, they remain the best children.

# Waiting for Trash Day

When I was a preschool teacher, trash day was an event every Tuesday and Thursday. The preschoolers would gather at 10:00 in the morning for recess. When they heard the noise of the large garbage truck entering the parking lot, they would rush to the fence. The fence divided the large parking lot from the nursery school. We teachers followed, though we didn't run. We knew they were safe, but we still wanted to keep a close watch. Sometimes, the children's screams and shouts were louder than the truck hauling the large trash containers.

We had trash day twice a week due to the abundance of disposable diapers, tissues, and paper that needed to be taken to the dump site. Now, I reside in a senior citizen apartment building where trash day is also significant. We don't want to miss it! The trucks come only once a week. From my window, I can see the maintenance staff taking the containers down the street. Sometimes, we forget to take out our trash the day before, and on the morning of trash day, we find ourselves chasing the truck driver down the street!

Occasionally, when a resident passes away, their relatives or loved ones hurry to fill the large bin with the belongings of the departed. The precious items we cherished in life end up in the trash bins. But don't mourn for me, Argentina; I'm in a better place now. My abode is filled with books. I don't have to stop reading to cook or eat. I'm not bound by an alarm clock to remind me of going to work! Today, I'm reading the last chapter of a 400-page book, large print of course! A fantastic library book! The book is so good, so exciting that I don't need to pause for anything, not even for trash day.

# Young and Beautiful Girl is Singing

Have you ever heard the song "Wind Beneath My Wings"? It's a beautiful piece performed by Bette Midler. My daughter Rose would sing it repeatedly as a young girl. She even performed it at a school event once, shining brightly as she sang. Her bravery amazed me; how could such a young girl possess so much courage? In my home country of Mexico, I once sang in front of an audience. They enjoyed my performance and invited me back to sing on a television show the following week.

It was a program featuring children singing songs for children. However, fear held me back, and I never returned for the recording. To this day, I ponder the reason for my absence. Was it the fear of singing on camera, or the embarrassment of not having another dress besides the one I wore on Sunday? My daughter sang all through high school, and I believed she would pursue a career in music. Instead, she entered the accounting field and now works at a highly esteemed firm.

Like me, she set aside her singing. Sometimes, we must sacrifice our passions to make a living. She spends her days immersed in numbers; I spend mine teaching people the difference between 'snake' and 'snack.' Nowadays, her singing is confined to her car or the shower. She's young, beautiful and vibrant, and I hope she'll return to singing for an audience one day. Our lives shouldn't be devoid of music just because we're busy. We may not be able to reclaim our youth, but we can reintroduce music into our lives, for it is a vital part of our existence.

# Index for My Poems

# An Indomitable Mother

I gave a gift to a bastard…
I gave him a gift from heaven!
Two small children who today cry inconsolably!
You left one afternoon, you didn't say anything…

You disappeared and I was left with nothing.
Nobody consoles me!
I'm abandoned…
I'm not a widow!

I don't deserve anything!
I swallowed my pride and I took them to school.
I went to a sewing factory; I would work during the day.
In the dark night, I lulled them to sleep while I weep!

I sang them songs that they adored.
They don't have a father anymore!
But they will always have a mother!
A mother who will never give up!

# Alive

The damage is done, yet we remain alive.
Painful memories persist in our wake.
Do we conceal them?
Or release them into the ether?

Together, let's forge a new future.
Together, let's relearn the steps to stride forward.
Indeed, the damage is done...
But we are alive!

# Books and Dinosaurs

Rich people buy books without looking at the price.
Poor people don't buy books because they don't have money.
The rich and the poor are, so different, from each other.
In one of them, there is everything, nothing is missing.

In the other one, there is nothing and everything is missing.
Two worlds that will never meet because the rich…
They will never live in poverty!
The poor only in dreams will have riches.

This is a world where dinosaurs became extinct!
But in which poverty will never be extinguished!
Can books, do the miracle of escaping poverty?
They say that Sor Juana once had 4,000 books.

I want to give away 4,000 books, one day!
And thus help to extinguish poverty!
How can you help to extinguish poverty?
How can we make students to read again?

Bury them and be Happy
It sounds so easy, but I know is very difficult.
All that bitterness let them go.
You have suffered so much that your heart,
It's full of sorrows.

Pretend that you have been born again...
With a new heart that does not know of suffering.
In your new heart, there should be only room for joy and love.
The medicine for pain is time and forgetfulness.

Be happy, you have found yourself again!
Like when you came into this world...
But today you can choose:
Bury them and be happy!

# Dreamers

They say the world is full of dreamers!
And I say we need even more.
To dream about a better life for all…
To dream about unity and brotherhood.

To dream of peace amidst war,
To dream; the one who lived two millennia ago
Still dreams with us now!
Join me in this dream brothers and sisters.

Let's awaken the world…
With a call for more dreamers!

# Dancing

The girl went dancing.
It was a Saturday night.
She wanted to dance and have fun!
She wanted to play at being a woman.

Playing at being a woman…
She became a woman!
That night, the girl lost her childhood!
Nine months later…

She was given a cage as a home!
Playing at being a woman…
The girl became responsible for two lives.
Playing at being a woman…

The girl found a friend, a friend for life.
Playing at being a woman…
The girl has taught us to be better!
And take good care of our wonderful girls!

# Domestic Violence Survivor

I have a smile on my face.
But my heart is bleeding...
No, I am not an actress.
I am a survivor of domestic violence!

Why me?
I ask the heavens?
Why me?
I ask the wind?

The answers never came!
The answers are forbidden to me!
My own illness cannot be seen.
My own illness doesn't exist for the living!

How can I wish to die, in this land of plenty?
What's wrong with me!
I am tired of this life...
I don't have anybody to live for.

They want me to keep living.
But the living, don't have a place, for me!
I am a survivor of domestic violence
I couldn't change for them!
Why should I change for you?

# Everettes' Song

Perhaps you've heard some of these words in a song before.
Maybe they've been spoken to another soul.
All I know is that when Everett enters the classroom,
His smile brightens the entire room.

He's amiable, compassionate, and unfamiliar with deceit.
He shares his toys unconditionally.
Seeing Everett fills my heart with a myriad of feelings.
How can one student effect such a profound change?

The change from sorrow to joy!
The change from the desire to teach to the urge to resign!
Everett stands out; he's one of a kind!
Everett eagerly awaits my lessons!

You might have heard these words before,
But they're distinct this time because...
They compose Everett's song.
The song for: A nice and happy child.

# Giving Away Love

The two cats did not want her.
They did not know her...
They were frightened by her presence.
They wanted to stay away from her.
She was not intimidated, and a strategy was planned.
She used to say nice words to them.
She caressed their little paws.
She sang in the house; she took care of the plants.
She left them gifts, here and there.
Some tiny balls that they chased...
Some skeins of yarn that they destroyed!
She never got angry; she gave them smiles.
After a while, the cats were friendly.
No more scares or upsets!
No more hiding and scratching!
Give love today, and tomorrow...
You will see, the cats sitting down: with her!

# Her Eternal Resting Place

After the drama, comes calm.
After crying, comes a healing sleep…
It seemed like, she had lost him.
She was sure that this time, he would leave.

And that he would never return!
The following month, he returned.
He asked me for forgiveness.
He asked me for another chance.

We lived happily, for a while.
One day, hell returned again…
He yelled at me, threatened me, hit me.
Today, he spends his time crying…

He is in a mental hospital, for having killed her.
After the drama, comes calm.
After crying, comes a healing sleep…
After the drama comes calm.

Note from author: This poem was based on a real life story. I have written the poem to honor the memory of two wonderful mothers. They gave their lives for their own children. They are real martyrs in these violent times of domestic violence. This horrible tragedy happened in 1983 in Val Verde, California.

# Hidden Kindness

"I don't want to know what day it is today!
I don't want to know where I'm going!"
"What is hurting you?"
The doctor asked him "because I can't see your pain."

My soul aches from so much disappointment
My soul aches from so much corruption
Human lives are so many…
Human lives are not worth a penny!

They are not even worth that!
"I'm sick" says, the rich man to the doctor.
"Sit down, sit down", answered the doctor.
"Will you give me medicine?

Will I be cure very soon?
I have to make a lot of money!
I can't waste a day".
He is very ill, needs a kidney and a heart.

"These are the models to choose, dear fellow."
"I like this one and this one," says the sick man.
The following month the rich man leaves the hospital.
"A little coin," a beggar, asked, him as he passes by.

His new heart skips a beat!
"Who is asking for a coin?" asked, the rich man.
He looks at the beggar's face, and the rich man…
Recognized his father!

"Father, my father, don't you recognize me?"
"Sir, I don't have any children.
The only one I had…killed himself, last month.
He couldn't face so much poverty."

"I have his kidney and heart and with them: his kindness.
That kindness that I did not know…exist.
I won't give you a coin; I'll give you… a palace.
In that palace, all your homeless friends will live!"

Author's note,
When the rich become poor, they will now how it is!
When they won't have food!
When they won't have shelter!
When they won't have money for doctors!
When they won't have money for medicines!
When they won't have resident legal papers and their parents are dyeing!
When they won't have a wife or husband to kiss good night!
When they won't have a chauffeur to driving them around!
When their grown children are dying of drugs overdose!
When they have to burn books to warm themselves!
When airplanes will no longer fly because there is no more fuel!
When it won't be enough air to breathe!

# I'm Still Standing

Today may have brought me down... with the loss of my job.
Today may have brought me down... as I lost my home to foreclosure.
Today may have brought me down... seeing my husband sent to prison.
Today may have brought me down... knowing I can't attend school next year.

Today may have brought me down... as I have only bad news to share.
Yet, amidst these trials,
I stand resilient, prepared to battle once more.
Indeed, there is hope as long as we live.

Indeed, there is the possibility of a new home...
A new job, and visits to my husband in prison.
I will rest today, for tomorrow promises a lengthy day.
Don't write me off just yet... for I am still standing.

# Kelly

I named you after a princess, hoping...
You'd outshine the stars in the night dark sky!
My little girl grew up to challenge me, learning from my mistakes...
And instead of offering support, she met me with such disdain!
She's a rebel, mirroring my own turbulent youth...
We both battled against the norms, trying to mend a wrong!
Against the expectative of our own history: women are failure.
Wanted to be; my own golden anchor in future tough times.
My daughter was meant to be my future...
Yet, we both dwell in wars of bygone days.
For us, the present and past merge.
She and I, share a common adversary: ourselves.

# Leaving in Fear

What went wrong between us, you and me?
Thirteen years have flown by,
So much water has flowed under the bridge.
You've witnessed many tears shed,
Fights with your father in the past,
And now, the battles are with you!
Your father departed years ago...
I toiled away for endless hours.
Leaving you feeling like an orphan...
Without parents and without a home.
Forgive me if I've wronged you.
I yearn for my baby to return!
The one I once rocked to sleep!
Let's cease the fighting today.
And repair our bond...
Your father may be gone,
But I remain here with you.
Let's discard our rage today.
Bury the violence!
That shakes our existence.
Let's give ourselves a new opportunity.
Indeed, you are thirteen, no longer a child...
Yet not quite a man!

# Life

Life can be tough, and at times, it seems unfair.
Why do some dine with silver cutlery?
While others must, plead for a meal?
How can we transform this world for the better?
For ages, idealists have endeavored:
Proclaiming against injustices,
Struggling to reform society,
Devoting years to the education of youth,
Investing years in nurturing virtuous offspring,
Upholding their ideals... some even became martyrs.

# Like the Tide

She ebbed and flowed like the tide, coming and going.
At forty, she is in the prime of her life...
While I at seventy, wish to end mine!
As I bid her farewell...
My heart yearned to never let her go.
With two daughters to nurture and a husband to love!
Her life is full of flowers and the moon shines upon her!
I returned to my small room in tears...
My life is empty without her smile...
She has departed like the tide!
And I am certain, she will not return to stay.

# Let Us Go

Just because she has ovaries
Is she supposed to bear children?
Just because I have a mother and she cooks…
Am I supposed to be like her?
Just because she is beautiful!
Is she supposed to cover…
Her beautiful body, from head to toe?
Just because I am not allowed to preach…
I should not preach?
Helen Keller was blind and she wrote books.
Harriet Tubman was born as a slave…
But she gave freedom to 300 slaves.
Sor Juana was a famous poetesses and nun in Mexico,
But not even the convent could stop her,
From writing her beautiful poems.
Let us go and we will lead.
Let us go and we will show,
Because a woman's destiny
Should not ever be written by the hands of men!
Their destiny is written in the stars, by God.
Let us go because this is our time.

# Mexico

A sacred place, bestowed upon the Aztecs by their deities.
It was nestled between two majestic volcanoes.
It was supposed to be an enchanted land.
The tears Mexico sheds today could fill a new lake.
This hallowed ground has been desecrated…
By the criminal hands that slay Mexican women and children.
Where are the gods who once led the Aztecs?
Our hope fades as we behold this terrible, terrible slaughter.

# Money, Money, Money,

Roll, roll, and roll, then nestle in my pocket snug.
I vow to cherish you with care.
For Mom, some earrings I shall procure.
For Dad, tools that are sure to endure!
And for myself, books to explore galore!
What treasures will you secure with your money's lore?

# Monday

Thank god for Monday
I love you Monday
You ask me why?
Because on Monday!
The children go back to school!

# My Own Time

I am here to share my story.
Some may not wish to listen!
For I am not recounting jokes...
I am speaking of my sorrows!
The melancholic life of a poor woman.
Overlooked, for being one among many.
For years, I toiled in a sewing factory.
For years, I labored in the onion fields.
For years, I cleaned the homes of the rich!
I remained unseen...
A specter yearning to vanish!
I was mute!
I had nothing to voice!
My husband was a man of madness!
Many recognized his malevolence.
Yet, no one extended a hand to rescue me!
I never ventured places by myself...
Afraid of shadows and dark roads!
My children follow me...
From their school, we returned home.
From home, I proceeded to work!
I perpetually awaited my moment.
Like a captive anticipating release!
At last, that moment came...
Dear God, my pleas were acknowledged!
I possess a voice and a tale to narrate!

# My Basket

In my basket, I don't have fruit or bread.
In my basket, I only have books to give away!
Books to have fun while reading them:
Monday, Tuesday, and Wednesday.
Books to learn while reading them:
Thursday, Friday and Saturday.
On Sunday, I will fly a kite!
Books for children because they just start to live.
Books for an old man because he is afraid of his future.
Books for women, so they can own their future!
Come for your book and start dreaming!
Come for your book and open windows to your world!
Come for your book and kiss your ignorance goodbye.
In my basket, I don't have fruit or bread.
In my basket, I only have books to give away!

# Pain

Sometimes it is very hard to believe that
The pain is going to be over and...
Tomorrow promises to be a better day.
We endure the pain, a tangible agony,
Comparable to the throes of childbirth,
Or the sharp assault of a stabbing.
Such a dreadful, piercing knife...
Yet heartaches remain unseen,
Felt deeply within...
Some will never comprehend this anguish.
Fortunate are they!
I am acquainted with this pain!
I am familiar with endless days of tears...
No solace found for my suffering.
How does one halt it?
How does one escape?
Still, we place our trust,
Handing our hearts over
To those who shatter them into countless shards.
And in the aftermath,
No one is present to ease...
This excruciating unbearable pain!

# Passing By

As I pass by, I feel compelled to share what I've witnessed.
A teacher endeavors to educate,
A poet strives to inspire change,
A journalist pens what may be his final piece.
You might wonder:
In which era did this occur?
Was it the 1800s, resistant to change?
Or the 1900s, clamoring for it?
No, my friend, it is our own century.
These are the modern times, hailed as the best.
We boast computers and smart phones.
Yet, something vital is absent.
Family values have dwindled; dismissed as obsolete.
The journalist met his end for merely doing his duty.
The teacher's wisdom is overshadowed by the allure of computers.
The poet's voice is silenced; their messages unwanted.
Darkness prevails,
For in these modern times, the light is unwelcome.

# Let's Drink Together

Give me one more tequila shot,
To forget the past that is always in my present.
Give me one more shot,
To stop my demons, they always follow me around.

Give me another shot,
To silence the voices of the ones, who once were my friends,
But these days they only live in my memories.
This bottle is my only friend.

She is the only one, by my side, all the time.
My other friends left me, the day that I gave up on my life.
Give me one more delicious tequila shot.
To forget what I know...I will never forget!

# Someone Like Me

If you lack humility, I possess it.
If you lack love, I offer it.
If you lack care, I provide it.
If you choose not to be someone like me,
I comprehend...
For once, I was someone like you.

# The World

I am just a woman
What can I do?
I am just a woman
Don't give me the World!

I am just a woman
I might change things
I am just a woman
Love and compassion

I maybe bring…
I am just a woman
Are you ready for me?

# The Rain

He labors with his hands from dawn to dusk...
He is unperturbed by rain, his duties must be fulfilled!
A solitary silhouette against the skyline...

He is gripping a hammer in his strong hands.
Feet perched high above the earth!
His toil is ceaseless, his motives a mystery...
The only certainty is the wonderful view from my pane!

A solitary silhouette on top of the neighboring roof!
We may never shift mountains with our bare hands,
Nor bear the weight of tons upon our shoulders...
We may never journey to the sun to drape our garments upon its fiery snout.

Yet, we can compose a melody that stirs the hearts of multitudes.
We can craft tales that draw laughter or tears.
We can devise marvels to rescue lives or traverse to distant worlds.
Our minds, weighing less than three pounds, with proper nurture...

Can transport us beyond the stars...
All without lifting a finger.

# True Lies

Whom can I trust?
I search everywhere
And couldn't find anyone worthy.
Each person is engaged in the same deception.

Like children in a game of hide and seek,
Adults lie with conviction.
Convinced their falsehoods...
Will never return to haunt them!

They lie so often that their lies
Are somehow parts of their life?
Convinced their falsehoods...
Will never return to haunt them!

# Too Many Children

As a little girl, I never owned toys.
My mother instructed me to care for her babies
while she tended to the dirty laundry.
She laid them in my small arms.
I yearned to tell her that I was just a child,
that I longed to play with my peers,
with kids my own age.
I bestowed upon my little sisters all my love and care.
I ensured they were nourished, clean, and secure.
Through my guidance, they learned to read and write.
Through my example, they learned to emulate me.
Six sisters arrived, each as lovely as a rose.
At last, a boy was born.
He arrived when I was fifteen.
My baby brother resembled baby Jesus,
so gentle, so exquisite.
My mother, swamped by the multitude of children,
depended on my assistance, as did my siblings.
My history fuels my storytelling and poetry,
some pieces hold a special place in my heart.
This poem about my family is one such piece.

# The Drums

The drums are calling your name and mine!
In a distant land someone needs us
"What should I bring with me?"
You may ask.
A knife, a gun, a sword perhaps?
Nothing like that!
Don't worry lad…
This is a new war, as you can see.
People have stopped reading!
They also have stopped writing!
They ignored the calls of the wise.
Who needs to read?
Who needs to write?
We are having so much fun.
Pick up a book, and come with us!.
The rebels are laughing because
They don't know how much they are missing!
They are losing so much… living in darkness.
The mighty pen will conquer them…Once again!

# The Same Song

For as long as live,
I will sing the same song!
My own children are tired of me…
This bird was hurt for life.

They don't want to hear my song anymore!
My two friends also tell me the same thing.
I keep singing the same song.
This bird was hurt for life

These wounds will never heal!
They are wounds in my heart.
They are open wounds and poison my blood.
This bird was hurt for life.

I keep singing the same song.
I don't have another one…
I must close my eyes to love!
This bird was hurt for life.

# Queen for a Day

I yearn to be a queen for just one day,
To issue commands, not just obey,
To act as I wish, not as I must.
Alas, the crown of a queen is not just for me.

Born into poverty, my sole desire is to hold onto a dream.
Born a woman, destined to tidy and cook,
While my books gather; dust and decay.
I await the day my wish becomes reality.

I covet not wealth or precious metals.
My wish is for a day of liberty to read and write,
As others tend to the cooking and cleaning, for me…
The Queen!

# Walking

Her screams were unheard.
Her pain was unseen.
She walked by day,
And she walked by night.

Awaiting her was another world,
A place devoid of sorrow,
A place devoid of pain.
Her pain has vanished, yet sadness remains,

Her everlasting companion…
She mourned for someone dearly missed,
an innocent child never brought to life,
a sweet child her arms will never embrace.

She accepted America as her new abode,
And America welcomed her as its new offspring.
Weary, she yearns for rest,
But rest is not yet within her reach.

Many others share her plight…
Many others in need of aid!
They walk by day and by night,
Silencing their screams and concealing their pain.

# Watching the Dream of an Angel

I'm going to watch the night.
I will sleep during the daytime.
I will ensure that nothing happens to you.
I see your angelic face.

You sleep, while, I listen to your little musical box.
I don't get tired of what I do.
You are my whole life.
You are my great treasure.

Little daughter of mine, never grow up...
I will never let the world hurt you.
You are my whole life.
You are my great treasure.

Printed in the United States
by Baker & Taylor Publisher Services